AFTER MODERN ARCHITECTURE

1995
1000
CP

PAOLO PORTOGHESI

AFTER
MODERN
ARCHITECTURE

RIZZOLI
NEW YORK

First published in the United States of America in 1982 by

RIZZOLI INTERNATIONAL PUBLICATIONS, INC.,

712 Fifth Avenue, New York NY 10019

Copyright © 1980 Gius. Laterza & Figli, Spa, Italy

ISBN: 0-8478-0408-9

LC: 81-51379

Translated from the Italian by Meg Shore
Composition by Interstate Graphics, Arlington, Vermont
Printed and bound by Kingsport Press,
Kingsport, Tennessee

TABLE OF CONTENTS

Look, we don't love like flowers, with only a single
season behind us; immemorial sap
mounts in our arms when we love. Oh, maid,
this: *that we've loved, within us, not one, still to come, but all*
the innumerable fermentation; not just a single child,
but the fathers, resting like mountain-ruins
within our depths. . .

R.M. RILKE, *The Third Elegy*

FOREWORD

This book is especially useful for two reasons: first, because it deals with recent events on both sides of the Atlantic as they are related to a common movement, the international reaction against canonical modernism in architecture; and second, because it stresses the pluralism of that movement and the multiplicity of its forms. It is salutary, after the intolerance of so much modernist theory, to realize that the works of Venturi and those of Rossi, for example, can be at once fundamentally linked and profoundly different—as are, in general, the European and American wings of the movement as a whole. In Europe the reaction against modernist iconoclasm and utopianism seems to have turned forcibly back toward that pervasive neo-classical tradition which has been the most tenacious force in European architecture since—one is tempted to say Augustan Rome—at any rate Palladio, and which has previously had two of its most intense manifestations at what might be called the two beginnings of the modern age: the first in the later eighteenth century, the second at the end of the nineteenth. Portoghesi's own work, like some of his finest historical studies, is in fact involved with a very different kind of style, one which is primarily Baroque in character. But the neo-classical tradition has been pervasive enough in Europe to be closely equated there with a more wholly vernacular architecture, of the kind which Europeans and Americans now seem anxious to identify and to employ once more. That vernacular has been associated in Europe with pre-industrial building methods and pre-capitalist social conditions. Leon Krier is most emphatic on these points when he says that architects must go back to the values of what he calls "Classical and Vernacular cultures."*

The American side of the movement has a somewhat different orientation. Differences in political philosophy play some rôle but in this case not a major one. The key factor lies in the American sense that the pre-industrial vernacular has already been adapted in America to industrial and capitalist usage, particularly by the Shingle Style of the late nineteenth century. This is not that the pre-industrial vernacular itself, with its special ties, by definition, to energy-efficient design, has not been of concern to the Americans of this generation. It is indeed central to much that is occurring right now. But it is significant that the present conscious rebellion against the limitations of European modernism began in America during the nineteen-fifties precisely with a revival of the Shingle Style. Of that general movement Louis I. Kahn was, it is true, the major precursor, but its derivation of direction from various architectures, like the Shingle Style, which were foreign to his interests, has caused the new American buildings to diverge farther from his work than have those of Neo-Rationalist Europe, upon which he must be considered a major influence as well.

Portoghesi explores the issues boldly, and with impressive culture, if not always in ways that will satisfy everyone. His reliance on some rather suspiciously late recruits to anti-modernism casts a shadow or two on his argument. All late converts are normally more fanatic than old believers, or wish to appear to be so. They are therefore not the

* Leon Krier, *Drawings 1967-1980*, Brussels, 1980.

most reliable sources for the facts on either side.

Again, hyper-nomenclaturism, so amusingly exploited by Charles Jencks and toward which Portoghesi is respectful enough, should in fact be employed with restraint, especially when it is linked to an analysis of form which is largely linguistic and associational rather than empathetic in character. Categorization is, after all, a minor critical virtue, if a real one. The question therefore arises whether Portoghesi's title is in fact a correct one, and whether what is going on is not, from any historical point of view, simply another aspect of modern architecture itself. To assume less is to equate modern architecture simply with the International Style, which was never a fact. To assume less, too, seems to release the present movement from the artistic necessity of commenting on the present, which—though it represents a welcome reaction to the *zeitgeist* cant of the German modernists—could be a crippling intellectual loss to us all.

Another issue arises. Anti-modernism has begun to attract the support of a number of journalistic popularizers and reactionary enthusiasts. The fact that the International Style was not a true political movement, and indeed came to serve Mammon more pervasively than it had ever served Marx, is irrelevent to the point, which is that anti-modernism may well be on the point of exploitation into a more or less effective mode of class war, as the Nazis used it. While this has been going on, "modernism" itself has found equally fatuous support in recent critical journalism, which points to its timeless "lessons" in space and structure and decries the more complicated cultural messages that are embodied in many of the recent forms. Serious architects and critics, who in fact care about art and who therefore do not see the issue in any of these reductive terms, should now be especially careful to make their meaning clear—or perhaps one should better say complex and contradictory. "If you can bear to hear the truth you've spoken twisted by knaves to make a trap for fools" has special meaning at the present time. The critic cannot control the disreputable uses to which his opinions may be put, but he should not permit the misrepresentation of his ideas to pervert them in fact, or to distort his own view of their validity. Truth is difficult. It often seems to be extremely complicated, as the present movement in architecture so bravely recognizes.

It seems obvious, too, that the critic should now repeatedly reaffirm the fact that the International Style itself was in its day a noble and heroic movement, one which created some magnificent buildings, as well as a revolutionary new image of the environment as a whole. That image has indeed swept the world and has, by its very nature, been profoundly destructive as well. It is against the destructive (and reductive) aspects of modernism that the present movement is largely directed. One of its primary aims is to bind up the urbanistic wounds that modernism has created, and to heal them as well as it can. This book plays an honorable part in that endeavor.

VINCENT SCULLY

Mario Ridolfi, De Bonis House, Terni, 1972–75.

Robert Venturi, drawing for a bank project, Fairfield, Connecticut, 1977.

Robert Venturi and Short, house, Chestnut Hill, Pennsylvania, 1962–64 (photograph by F. Moschini).

Ignazio Gardella, apartment house, Zattere, Venice, 1957.

ABOVE AND BELOW:
Venturi & Rauch, exterior and interior views, Brant–Johnson House, Vail, Colorado, 1976–77.

Charles Moore and Associates, Kresge College, University of California at Santa Cruz, 1974.

Charles Moore with Richard Chylinski, Burns House, Santa Monica, California, 1974.

Bruno Reichlin and Fabio Reinhardt, Sartori House, Riveo,
Ticino Canton, 1976–77.

Charles Moore and Associates, Piazza d'Italia, New Orleans,
Louisiana, 1977–79.

Bruno Reichlin and Fabio Reinhardt, Tonini House, Torricella,
1972–74.

S. Anselmi and P. Chiatante (GRAU), Parabita Cemetery, Lecce
1966-67.

Aldo Rossi, "Teatro del Mondo" enroute from Fusina to
Venice, 1979 (photograph by G. Massobrio).

Paolo Portoghesi, Giampaolo Ercolani, Giovanna Massobrio
consultant: M. Barlattani, COBASE eco-energy plan, thermal baths
Canino, 1978-80. (Project modified without permission of COBASE
cooperative).

Robert A. M. Stern and John Hagmann, Westchester house, Armonk, N.Y., 1974–76.

Paolo Portoghesi, Giampaolo Ercolani, Giovanna Massobrio and Associates, Academy of Fine Arts, Aquila, 1976–78.

Gianluigi D'Ardia, architectural drawing, 1979.

Robert A. M. Stern, Lang House, Washington, 1973–74.

Robert A. M. Stern and John Hagmann, interior view, Pool House, Greenwich, Connecticut, 1973–74.

Robert A. M. Stern, detail, Lang House, Washington, 1973–74.

Hans Hollein, travel agency, Vienna, 1978.

Robert Matthew, Johnson–Marshall and Partners, civic center, Hillingdon, London, 1978.

Christian de Portzamparc, water tower, Marne-La-Vallée, 1971–75.

Thomas Gordon Smith, perspective view, Long House, Carson City, Nevada, 1977.

Georgia Benamo and Christian de Portzamparc, rue des Hautes-Formes, Paris, 1975.

Michael Graves, drawing for the Fargo/Moorhead Culture Center Bridge, Fargo, N. Dakota and Moorhead, Minn., 1977–79.

Taft Architects, Utily District, Quail Valley, Texas.

Michael Graves, Sunar Furniture Showroom, New York, N.Y., 1979.

Charles Jencks, Garagia Rotunda, Wellfleet, 1977.

Thomas Beeby, drawing from "The House of Virgil built in expectation of the return of the Golden Age," 1976.

AFTER MODERN
ARCHITECTURE

THE TRAIL OF ASHES

"Art places life in disorder," wrote Karl Kraus at the beginning of this century, adding for the sake of clarity: "The poets of humanity are constantly reestablishing chaos." Just a few pages later in *Pro domo et mundo* there is another aphorism which seems to undermine the previous statement: "Only in the delight of linguistic generation does chaos become a world." The apparent incapability of the two propositions can help one understand the dramatic situation in which the architecture world finds itself today—divided between the necessity of breaking with its recent past and the temptation to draw from it the primary materials for building its future.

An artist—but the discussion would be equally valid for a group or a generation of intellectuals—needs chaos to put his ideas into effect; he needs a disjointed reality, beset by doubt. He needs to place in disorder the structured inventory of his inheritance which compels him to "make do," thereby paralyzing his action, even if the final end toward which he moves, unwittingly or not, is the passage from "chaos" to "world," from necessary disorder to a new order.

The architectural production of that which we euphemistically call the "civilized" world, and which we unilaterally identify with the industrial world, notwithstanding the confusion and the diversity of the phenomena which characterizes it, exhibits a high degree of condensation and monotony. It conforms to consolidated principles, realising over the last forty years a homolgizing process of cosmic dimension, reaching beyond every geographic limitation to impose the same standards upon the most diverse cultures, thereby cancelling out their individual identities.

"Modern architecture"—which in its actual architectural production consists of its conventions, its dogmas, its grand experiences; the great archetypal model, corrupted and betrayed in interpretation, as a kind of sacred text, and yet always followed and obeyed in the ultimate reading—has been on trial for a long time. But it has withstood successive waves of attacks, continuing to oppose them with a barrier of indifference, supported by a solid alliance with power, as a result of its identification with the productive logic of the industrial system.

In this attempt to consolidate itself as a permanent and immutable tradition, inextricably bound to industrial society, modern architecture has provided itself with a statute, unwritten but functioning and binding in reality, the observation of which is stubbornly defended by the powerful establishment of official criticism. We could define this as the "functionalist statute." This statute is not, as we will see, the ingenuous formulation of a principle which once affirmed the dependent relationship between form and function which, in fact, serves neither to distinguish modern from ancient architecture, nor to guarantee modern architecture a continuity of development. This statute is, rather, a collection of prohibitions, curtailments, renunciations, inhibitions one could say, which define in the negative a linguistic area, allowing for a degradation, a drying up, a continuous metamorphosis, but not for a substantial renewal or a vital return.

In order to understand the curious impasse in which modern architecture finds itself it is useful to schematically review its genesis in the early decades of this century. There emerges a sort of Oedipal complex, tying today's architecture to that of the preceding culture and constituting its hidden impetus and historic justification. The resolution of this Oedipal complex, with the death of the embattled father, has definitively denied to modern architecture the cohesion which gave a sense of unity to other movements. This "killing of the past" has released a spring, setting off a reaction against the dogmatism of tradition, but transforming its anti-dogmatism into a new and sterile restriction.

From this metaphor one could go on to say that for modern architecture the hated father was historicism, first Neo-classicism, then Eclecticism, both of which characterized the early period of bourgeois architecture. In opposition to this phase, whose mimeticism reflected the "spirit of the time," in which the industrial epoch masked its features behind the riches of preceding civilizations—modern architecture claimed the necessity of a new style, corresponding to new demands and new ideas. At first this problem of a new style gave birth to a series of attempts which did not forego the developmental continuity of architecture as a human institution. The principle that one type of architecture is transcended by another had yet to be espoused. Instead, themes were developed which had their roots in the historic construction of architectural "institutions." In the second and third decades of this century, however, even these links were drastically called into question. Architecture which obeyed the functionalist statute was born, as it were, by parthenogenesis; not from existing architecture, which represented the slow accumulation of experiences produced by mankind within a defined tradition, but from an analytic process, which was purged of every intentional historic or symbolic contamination.

The first phase, from the 1880s to 1910, which tended more modestly to the construction of a new style, corresponds to the creative eclecticism of Labrouste, Richardson, Eiffel and Norman Shaw and to the international phenomenon of "modernism," from Art Nouveau (Liberty Style in Italy) to Expressionism and to Art Deco. The second, more radical phase corresponds to Rationalism in its numerous forms, and everything which derives from it, from the International Style to Neo-Brutalism.

Naturally, hatred for and destruction of the father pertain exclusively to the second phase: so-called Rationalism or Functionalism and its derivatives. The radical and explicit attitude of this movement determined its impetus and destiny during the period between the two world wars and its passive resistance during the post-war period until today. All historical interpretation, at least until a few years ago, considered Rationalism evolutionistically, as a point of arrival, the synthesis of all preceding investigations, the definitive, concrete architectural expression of industrial society. It was not seen as a style in the traditional sense, for a style by its very nature can be substituted by another which follows. Instead it was seen as something beyond style, the definitive fulfillment of a program which cannot change, at least as long as industrial society exists.

To thoroughly purify its visible results, the functionalist statute prescribed an architecture which tended to regress from material to idea. At the origin of every spatial form it placed not the hut, as in the theoretical tradition of classicism, but geometry, the primary forms of the Euclidian universe and in particular, the cube, as the fundamental archetype, from which there can be extracted by simplification or successive aggregation, all the basic elements of the functional lexicon: the pilaster, the beam, the slab, the plane, the recess and the combination of any of these primary entities.

This radical choice interrupted a continuous process based on the recycling and creative transformation of any number of prototypes which had survived in the western world for centuries. As the continuity of linguistic institutions, from the time of Egyptian architecture onwards, this process had even resisted the dramatic collapse of political institutions in the ancient world. In reality, the destruction of morphological continuity was a revolution of forms which only partially corresponded to a revolution of methods and ideas. The result, as we shall see, was the creation of a culture incapable of evolution and renewal, destined (notwithstanding its attempts to substitute Euclidian with non-Euclidian geometry and elementary functionalism with psychological functionalism) to become an iron cage, a labyrinth without exit, in which a search for the new, for the different, has produced a tragic uniformity, a trail of ashes.

"In the sportive body, every harmonious part finds its destiny: the legs are made for the race, the thighs for the horse, the arms for the bow, the womb for love." This description[1] dates from the 1930s and refers to an ancient portrait of Diana de Poitiers, but it expresses perfectly the "functionalist" mode of thought which proceeds from a dissection of things into parts, and analysis which fragments reality, in search of its mental equivalent. This description, as Eugene Bafaumais has observed, tends to make us believe that "Diana would love less well and would be more proficient in her use of horses, bows, and men, had she been discovered in an unfragmented state." Rereading the theories of architectural functionalism, there emerges the same certainty—that every complex reality comes to be understood as one would understand a machine or a watch, taking it apart piece by piece. Since man there has been an operation of the body of the city, which has led to zoning, that is to say a system of subdividing it into areas and of attributing to each of these areas homogeneous, specialized functions. In this way architecture, having established certain urban spaces according to quantitative considerations, has become a redundant element, added to a predetermined urbanistic volume, like a sheet of colored paper used to wrap a Christmas gift.

Is it possible, that this analytic approach continues to exercise its deforming influence in a society which presumably has discovered the sterility of such an attitude and has adopted a "systemic approach" to face the problems of complexity, taking into account the totality of elements of the system, examining them in their interrelationships and interdependencies? Is it possible that a society which has questioned the very foundations on which the functionalist statute rests (that is, the authority of unshared knowledge and the certainty of being able to have a qualitative effect on the environment while operating only within restricted parameters such as hygiene, orientation, repetition) doesn't know how to shake off a paralyzing inheritance and thus limits itself, at best, to superficial attempts to adapt to new necessities?

1 "Remarques Anti-fonctionelles et irresponsables" by Eugene Bafaumais, *Traverses*, 4/1974, Editions de Minuit, Paris

The reasons for the stability and tough resistance of this methodology are numerous and profound, and this book will not assume to enumerate them in an organic or exhaustive fashion. It is sufficient to point out that, along with the complicity of the industrial system, based on profit at any cost and on a tendency to confront problems one at a time, there exists what one might call the hidden weapon, insidious and deadly. This is the ideology of the perpetually new, of change for its own sake. In its admiration of novelty, modification of means, materials and value judgments (whatever is new is valid insofar as it is the guaranteed product of invention, of a creative act), the Modern Movement has subscribed to it own self-perpetuation and irreplaceability. How can one, in fact, change something which by nature is in continuous flux? The very word "modern" expresses something continuously shifting, like the shadow of a person who is walking. How can one free oneself from one's shadow? It is not accident that the most courageous and radical critics of the Modern Movement have been constrained to choose that most awkward and paradoxical of adjectives— "post-modern"—to define their attitude. It is the only phrase which can clearly express a refutation of continuity.

THE POST-MODERN CONDITION

"Our working hypothesis is that the statutes of knowledge change when society enters the so-called post-industrial age and culture the post-modern. This passage began more or less at the end of the 'fifties. . .' "

JEAN-FRANCOIS LYOTARD, *The Post-Modern Condition*, 1979.

The idealistic philosophies which dominated aesthetic formulations of the last two centuries and which strongly conditioned the writing of architectural history have attributed a metaphysical value to the term "Architecture." It has thereby become a sort of seal of quality, setting apart those products built by man which contain traces of a conscious intellectual mediation between social exigencies and their translation into physical, resolved objects (be they projects or realized constructions). Having entered into the rarified garden of "art," architecture has thus become the product and the domain of the creative personality, separated from other forms of environmental production. All other aspects in this sector of human endeavor which are dedicated to the transformation of the environment have been judged by other criteria and placed in other categories, form the lesser arts to industrial design and city planning. Consequently, a considerable amount of environmental data has been excluded from disciplined historical studies and rather general critical investigations, leading to grandiose ideological formulations, have become the guiding principles which have animated the debate on architecture.

Among the phenomena which have remained in the shadows and one which merits particular attention are those productions of the building industry which are currently denied architecture's seal of quality, with a capital "A," but which nonetheless constitute the connective fabric of the modern city, or, more accurately, the tissue of the urban periphery. Along with this sprawl of "quantity without quality" and directly related to it, there looms the wealth of visual references which overlay the primary urban structure, extending a thick network of signs as the indispensable components of urban life. These make up a totality of interventions at varying scales, ranging from interior furnishings and street decoration, to commercial signs and graphics, and finally, to daily attire itself, which, with its ever increasing variability has become one of the most sensitive barometers of changing taste.

According to the old models of historical interpretation, these aspects of environmental reality were considered non-essential to the transformational genesis of architecture. They were seen, if at all, as usefully evoking the spirit of the epoch or as the visual reflections of a society, as the enervated by-products of a genuine "creative" activity. And so the urban phenomenon, in all its complexity, has remained largely unexplained: mere building, lacking monumental values and considered a degeneration and simplification of more cultivated models, has never been analyzed according to its rules of growth and its reality, in which institutional factors (linguistic conventions, distributive and formal typologies meet face to face with new collective and individual needs.

This simplification has led to an overestimation of the historical contribution of great creative personalities and to an underestimation or negation of local culture as this has contributed to the collective transformation of the city. This same simplification has been functional to the growth and development of the ideology of the Modern Movement, based on the claims of a small band of intellectuals from the most industrially developed nations who sought to establish a body of universal rules for the study of architecture which would guarantee a correspondence between the new method and the "spirit of the age." The ideology of the Modern Movement as the "functionalist statute" advanced as such in its schematic formulation in the 1920s was widely accepted and diffused without restraint, resulting in a supremacy of time over place and in the complete uprooting of the discipline from the material conditions of its origin and development.

Alternatively invoked as both art and "science," above individual judgment, contemporary architecture became the abstract pseudo-science of time, and it was an attempt at visually expressing new needs and new sensibilities after they had been analyzed, or rather, intuited, in a laboratory. In fact the result has been a loss of architecture's specificity and its capacity to mediate concretely between a society and its determined place.

During the period 1930-1960, the "stories" of the Modern Movement, inspired by the literary model of the historical novel, verified the basic hypothesis of the new architectural culture—either constructing a composite biography of an intellectual adventure, lived by the apostles of the new word—or being preoccupied with the relationship between changes in the methods of production and resultant changes in architecture itself. There was, however, a continuous failure to fully investigate the modification of the visual environment and its culture of images, the origins of which lay in the influence of a new reality upon collective consciousness and its production.

The lack of critical categories employed in the study of urban phenomena has brought about the frequent introduction, in the above mentioned "stories," of chapters on the expansion and planning of modern cities, failing to understand their material transformations at the level of the primary structures of the urban fabric, the elementary cells which make up the continuous story of the city with its characteristic elements: main thoroughfares, secondary avenues, piazzas, courtyards, etc.—all of which are closely analogous with the elements of a system of logic.

The history of the Modern Movement has been seen more or less in terms of a "star system," similar to that of the world of cinema in the 1920s and 30s with its focus on actors and directors. Le Corbusier, Gropius, Mies van der Rohe Wright,—all have been considered absolutely original inventors, linked in an evolutionary manner to the unfolding of a single tradition, the Modern Movement, reduced in its turn to a single phenomenon, stripped of the profound contradictions which make up its realised manifestations.

The task of the historians, according to this plan, seems to have been to definitively separate architecture from its material tradition (articulated so forcefully in specific geographic situations), so as to guarantee a unique and decisive link with man in the form of an explosive mix of individual creativity and pure technology.

Given the close connection between the ideology of the Modern Movement and its historical interpretation which it has created in its own image, one may speculate about the historiographic consequences which will be brought about by any abandonment of the modernist orthodoxy. How, for example, will the conquests, rebellions, moods, and the new aspects of civilization which characterize the last decades, be interpreted? Although the panorama of most recent changes in the world of architecture is increasingly complex, dispersive and contradictory, it is possible to note two aspects, the ever growing presence of which makes one think that there has been a radical turning point in the way one looks at architecture and generally links it in a more general sense to its past.

The first of these aspects is a suspicion of grand historical schemes and a tendency to verify the reliability of historic hypothesis through rigorous reconstruction of facts. This approach has dismantled piece by piece, the virtual pyramid of the Modern Movement, substituting in its place a multitude of small, differently oriented pyramids.

The second of these aspects is in the need to re-examine in conjunction with past and present events of "high culture," the commonplace events of our daily lives in the cities where we live, in the territories which we have transformed (so often destroying the identity and beauty). There is a need to somehow relate the two realities, abandoning the untenable posture of judging the Modern Movement too beautiful and perfect to have a place in this "Valley of Tears." One can no longer have faith in this thesis, according to which the Modern Movement would have best remained only in the blueprint stage, never to be judged for better or worse in the real world. On the contrary, one may assert that never before has a cultural blueprint (the product of an intellectual minority working in a restricted geographic area) exercised so strong and pervasive an influence, crossing every geographic and cultural boundary.

This relationship between the two architectural realities, the cultural and the banal, as well as the architectural environment as a whole, with its myriad of characteristic signs attesting to man's appropriation, speaks of a new mode of interpretation more than a new intuitive sensibility. There is an intensely political demand, which exploded in 1968, to substitute a sclerotic and illusory democracy, based on the delegation of power from the top, with a democracy controlled at the base, renewed by the consensus arising out of the mechanism of its organization. If the culture of '68 was corrupted by a pathetic attachment to Marxist orthodoxy and to a somewhat idealized conception of social classes, its vital forces did, however, set in motion systems of verification which broke the taboos behind which were entrenched the tradition of modern art, linked by many historians in all too mechanical fashion to ideals of revolution and progress.

Together with the impetus of '68 there was the new sociology, new contributions to psychopathology, psychoanalysis and semiology, and, more generally, new theories of information. These were available to historians and together they constituted the new intellectual tools for revising the role of avant-garde art. This revision still remains in large part unaccomplished, but the consequences of it are already being felt. The art of the avant-garde, born out of the intentional divorce of groups of intellectuals from the line of ruling, "official" taste, was for a time an attempt, both noble and pathetic, to maintain the qualitative elite aspects which characterized the cultural production of preceeding epochs. Then, the concentration of power had lain in the hands of a restricted ruling class, and the elaboration of cultural models was dependent on an alliance between this ruling class and "its" intellectuals and artists. The bourgeoisie's rise to power brought about, in earlier times, extraordinary dynamic attempts to define new relationships, whereby artists would align themselves, now with the petite bourgeoisie, now with the more "sensitive" stratum of the upper bourgeoisie. But there was never a stabile recreation of the alliance of power which had characterised the *ancien regime* except, in an illusory fashion, through official, state art of mediocre quality.

The avant-garde emerges from the refusal of intellectuals to recreate this relationship, but also from a nostalgia for the pre-industrial conditions in which intellectuals were assigned powerful roles in a cultural hegemony. There was a polarized tension or concern to tie the future itself to a social class which was destined to assume a new mythical hegemony—the nineteenth century proletariat, as described by Marx, were seen as heirs to the great cultural traditions of the West.

In this historical dilemma there is no place at all for the lower classes. The urban proletariat, uprooted and exploited, struggles for survival and certainly does not find itself in a condition in which it may establish an alternative culture. Rural civilization, drained by new exploitive ties to urban civilization, has come to be seen as a mirror of the past, as symbolic of submission and therefore as a patrimony to be rejected; or else it is seen as a romantic evocation of a paradise lost.

And so a cultural neutrality has been attributed to the class which was destined to free the world from oppression, to eradicate from the world the very principle of class divisions; but this neutrality robbed this class of any cultural inheritance. If the bourgeois revolution is the consequence of the cultural production of the ascending bourgeoisie, the proletariat revolution can be seen and projected as the ascent of a class without culture, or at least without culture other than that of struggle and desire.

This total removal of the lower classes from the field of cultural accomplishments was based on the concept of an intellectual culture drastically separated from "material" culture. This was not only intrinsic to a specifically bourgeois concept of class, but also a direct response to the realities of an industrial age, when great migrations from the country to the city erased the cultural identity of the migrant worker, without allowing for the growth of an alternative identity.

One hundred years later, with the continuous strategic transformation of class conflict and the evident osmosis between classes, with their fracturing into opposing groups, this process by which a class assumes power in terms of its own culture only to await its inheritence from the preceeding ruling class seems hardly now credible particularly since this class has in the meantime become the object of narcissistic self destruction. Similarly irrelevant is the odious role of a Shakesperian Iago, faithful to the petite-bourgeoisie, potential ally of reactionary forces and as detestable a figure as can be imagined in the field of culture and art.

In past civilizations the lower classes produced

culture, although not as an unmotivated autonomy, but rather, through employing the models and experiences of the ruling class and their cultural mediators, exhibiting above all a collective creativity "without name," as valid as the individual and "signed" works of the court or bourgeoisie; one which gave definition and meaning to a particular civilization. The substance and charm of lower class production—without which the relationship between culture and civic society would have remained incomplete and incomprehensible, did not go unnoticed by artists, who freely used the material produced by other epochs, from Homer to Mahler. In the field of architecture, however there was until recently an absence of instruments necessary to the accurate assessment of its role.

An entire generation of architects and historians was put to work, learning to "read countries" to networks created by the superimposition of successive inventions, the man-made agrarian landscapes. Only in this way could there emerge the full meaning of both city and country-side which, (contrary to the virtuoso symbolic concentrations of art tied directly to power), gives birth to a collective feeling for form which works in a creative manner over time. A streetscape, made up of adjacent houses, all of the same typology but from different eras, draws its meaning from a dialogue among diverse protagonists across the ages, all working on a single "project." This phenomena is deeply rooted in the collective conscience, tied in resolute fashion to real needs and desires. This long distance "dialogue" has characteristics similar to the creative process itself; it unfolds at the core of an individual's imagination and culture; it is the fruit of a collective critical activity similar to the self-criticism which leads an artist to tie together the different parts of a given work or to come upon different solutions for the same theme.

Let us consider a concrete example, the German village of Lamspring. Here there is a convergence of elements which while diverse are comparable in their homogeneity. Thus their elevational continuity defines the overall piazza-street configuration in order to yield an aesthetic effect which is the expression of a culture "without heroes"; a quality different from but not inferior to, that of the monument. The incapacity to gather together and rigorously analyze these qualities or the tendency to ambiguously classify them as picturesque products of nature, together with the inability to look at them in terms of the dominant culture, even if they remain in opposition to it—these are the consequences of a philosophy of art predicated on subservience to power.

Our goal is to define new methodological premises, new tools for understanding, adapted to the recognition and modification of a situation of growing complexity. The first tool is an awareness that, with the present ambiguous articulation of conflicting groups and social classes, it is illegitimate to attribute to any of them a monopoly on culture without belittling the term and turning it into an unconscious instrument to maintain privilege. On the contrary, it is necessary to recognize and analyze the identities of diverse cultures, including the "banal", and to study their inter-relationships.

The second instrument is the realization that there exists, together with individual output, a collective production of works of aesthetic interest and that, beyond a creative process linked to economic development and the cult of the personality, one must study those inter-personal processes which are mediated by institutions and social aggregations, both new and old.

The third tool is an awareness of the decisive effect on "high" culture of overall environmental transformations, including the most changeable and ephemeral facets of aesthetic production. These transformations, which are often the fruits of the reinterpretating new environmental conditions and forms—products which are not mediated by new needs and desires—also effect architecture with a capital "A."

The fourth tool is the discovery that industrial civilization has for a long time gone beyond its mature thresh-hold and can no longer be schematically represented by means of the symbols of its aggressive youth. The universe of the machine, with its enormous structures, its rigidly disciplined forms of organization, its productivistic and quantitative horizons, certainly remain a considerable factor in our civilization. But this universe is no longer sufficient to characterize our age *in toto* or to represent its vital energies and innovative tendencies. At present, industrial civilization can be seen as simultaneously contradictory and strongly dynamic; the "civilization of the machine" juxtaposes itself to (and attempts to integrate itself with) a culture of "limits" which tends to control the rhythms of autonomous industrial development, imposing on it a series of conditions.

In the face of the energy crisis, the loss of faith in technical development as the equivalent of social progress, and the loss of certainty that social revolution and a more advanced society awaits around the corner, today's world sustains two concurrent tensions, as opposing forces. There is often a confrontation between power concentrated in a few hands and an opposing power which pertains to the majority which is unable to identify its actual goals or to translate an awareness of its alienated condition into action.

A society thus divided can continue to display as triumphant symbols both the mechanical cog wheel and the exquisite, hermetic contrivance of the computer console. On the other hand, the most recent conquests of science deal not so much with the mechanical world as with the realm of information and communication. Those great electronic computers are not machines in the traditional sense of transforming energy, but rather, tools which work analogously to the human brain, elaborating and transforming information.

In this second or third stage of its life (be it maturity or old age), industrial society is divided in two and requires new symbols as well as a new sense of balance. The refutation of theories of unlimited growth have placed an accent, once again, on man and his daily life, on mass culture and its universe of forms, disregarding the images of the "cathedrals of work" which have, in any case, lost much of their fascination.

ARCHITECTURE AND
THE ENERGY CRISIS

The modern industrial system, this gigantic machine which unifies the most developed societies, overriding political systems and institutions, projecting a shadow of alienation over the worlds of both capitalism and "real" socialism, has built its power on foundations of clay which the passage of time has exposed. This system is based on the conviction that nature is an infinite entity from which one can limitlessly draw the energy necessary to power the "perpetual motor" of production. Now that it has become clear that the industrial system must pay its debt, not with its artificial capital but with another, non-replenishable capital—that of nature—the great myth of infinite development has collapsed. It has left in its place, however, an equally unproductive myth—that of crisis without resolution. After years of using natural capital as assured income, after having plundered the earth like a subjugated city, the system now prefers to embrace self-pity, and the ineluctable prospect of "the end of civilization," rather than a search for solutions or to examine nature in terms of a "new alliance," a relationship oriented toward a new equilibrium.

It is important to maintain the principle that nature can no longer be thought of as an infinite entity within which one sentimentally flounders, only to then plunderously turn upon it in the moment in which its resources are needed. Rather, it must be seen as a finite source in which one can understand the role of the eco-system comprised of human civilization, in relation to other eco-systems. Today's decisions will effect everyone's future, and of all the earth's riches, that which it is more criminal to deplete is the non-renewable environmental resources. More than a century ago, the socialist thinker, William Morris, warned the world not to forget this responsibility, and it is worthwhile to reread his exhortation:[1]

. . . each of us is duty bound to watch over and preserve the regulation of the earthly landscape, each with his spirit and his hands, in the portion that belongs to him, to avoid handing down to our sons a lesser treasure than that which was left to us by our fathers. There is no time to lose, leaving this problem unresolved to our final days so that our sons must resolve it; since humanity is impatient and greedy, and today's desires make us forget yesterday's resolutions; . . . we have enough time for everything: to populate the deserts; to break down frontiers between nations; to discover the most recondite secrets of the essence of our souls and our bodies, of the air which we breathe and the earth which sustains us; there is time to subjugate the forces of nature to our material power; but if we want to turn our attention and our curious desire to the beauty of the earth, there is not a minute to lose, in the fear that the continuous flux of human necessities will

1 From a speech given in London on March 10, 1881, on the subject of the Prospect of Architecture in Civilization, published in Italian translation in *Architettura e Socialismo*, Edizioni Laterza, Bari, 1963.

fall on it and render it not a desert of hope (which it once was), but a desperate prison; in the fear, finally, that we will discover that man has suffered, struggled, conquered and tamed all earthly things beneath his feet, only to make his very existence more unhappy."

It is not only Morris's "beauty of the earth" that is subject to ever increasing consumption. One realizes that architecture as well, seen as a second nature or as a reserve of accumulated experience has also become part of the drama since the "functionalist statute," adopted by advanced industrialism, assigns to the past, the explicit role of being a reservoir of value, and to the present the pure and simple role of managing this value.

There is no acknowledgment of the duty to offer a creative contribution to the "reserve" which, for its part, continues to be eroded by terribly destructive forces.

"Capitalism of development is dead. Socialism of development, which resembles it like a brother, confronts us with a deformed image, not of our future, but of our past. Marxism, although it remains irreplaceable as an analytical tool, has lost its prophetic value . . . We know that our present way of life has no future; that our future sons will no longer, in their old age, have at their disposal aluminum or oil; and that, in the case of the realization of nuclear projects, the reserves of uranium will be exhausted in their time . . . We know that our world is coming to an end and that if we continue as before, the seas and rivers will become sterile, the earth will be stripped of its natural fertility, the air of our cities stiffled and life reduced to a privilege for those who are selected champions of a new human race, adapted through chemical conditioning and genetic programming, to a new ecological niche synthesized for them by biological engineers."

These reflections by Andre Gorz, which begin his essay, "Ecologie e Liberté," have more than economic and political implications. They place in crisis one of the main principles of cultural prediction—the mythology of unlimited development. Modern architecture, which assumed its "definitive" configuration on the basis of this mythology during the period 1920 to 1970, has now entered a period of deep crisis from which it cannot extricate itself without taking an entirely new approach.

Until now the cultural world has reacted with indifference to the obsolescence of the guiding principles of the last fifty years of architecture, either feigning that nothing is the matter or at most admitting the need for some minor theoretical revisions. Only in the Anglo-Saxon world, which is less provincial and conformist, has there been an attempt to define the magnitude of the crisis, speaking of post-modern architecture and the "failure of modern architecture." Perhaps the most rational posture would be one that acknowledges that "modern architecture," as the style of an epoch, as the expression of technological civilization on the rise, is dead, and that the title "modern" now belongs to a different type of architecture, just as different as the "old modern" was from the Eclecticism which had preceded it.

Even a declining technological society, searching for salvation from the mortal consequences of its optimistic constructivist inheritance, will have its own architecture. But it is useless to try to revive a corpse or, worse, to enbalm it, as do certain diehards, especially in Italy. Working with the best intentions, and coming up with the most macabre results, they seek "continuity" at all costs.

As in any moment of transistion, however, we are at present confronted with a confusing and contradictory panorama. New facts are emerging like tiles of an incomplete mosaic, creating an unfinished figure, difficult to decipher. These phenomena, rejected by the old theories of the Modern Movement as disobedient heresies, scandalous evasions from the conservative orthodoxy, are the early symptoms of a process, the outcome of which cannot be predicted. What is already clear, however, is the obsolescence of much of the current architectural tradition, this pattern of knots whose disentanglement contains the beginning of a new method.

Architecture as a consumer good

The philosophy of the Modern Movement points toward a view of architecture as utilitarian object. Le Corbusier advanced the idea of the house as a "machine for living," and the objective to industrialize the building field has frequently been pursued with religious fervor. The distance from nature, the choice of artificial materials, the visual and functional relationship with the world of the machine—all these have been goals of the dominant tendency and have profoundly influenced the transformation of the earth and the new face of the city.

A civilization that is seriously concerned with the restoration of ecological balance and the conservation of resources cannot allow itself the luxury of continuing to build according to the old methods and ideals. The generalized use of metal, for example, with all its aesthetic and technological consequences, cannot be continued infinitely. Aluminum, used for the facing of millions of skyscrapers the world over, will soon become more rare than precious metal; nor are our iron reserves

unlimited. The prevalent use of metal parts in the maintenance of buildings is an even more unacceptable luxury. A masonry building has a life span and a rate of obsolescence measurable in centuries, demonstrated by the fact that we still live in cities built in the Middle Ages. A modern building, on the other hand, is already decrepit and its corroded parts in need of replacement after only thirty or forty years of use. Architects, abandoning roofs and cornices, have displayed arrogant indifference to atmospheric effects, especially rain. They have generated an ephemerally youthful architecture, incapable of aging with dignity, an architecture that one changes like a dress or a car, so as not to seem out of fashion.

The picture of energy consumption is even more tragic. Heating a house with stone walls and proportionate windows uses one tenth the energy needed to heat a glass, lightly insulated house. In this regard it would be hard to find a more irrational example than the glass skyscraper invented in the 1950s, and still widely accepted as the exemplary building type for offices. In fact, the substitution of external walls with a transparent diaphragm enormously increases the permeability of heat and cold and the rapid variability of temperature during the day. In order to compensate for this defect, not only is energy consumption increased, but mechanical systems are overbuilt to handle the rapidity of temperature variation. In addition, the lighting systems impose costly periods of partial and brief darkness, contributing to the rapid aging of the building.

Modern architecture, born out of a reaction to the useless waste manifested in the artificial decoration of nineteenth century Eclecticism and then adopted by ascendant capitalism as an ethic of austerity and simplicity, has paradoxically become an architecture which is wasteful of energy. It has become a gigantic mechanism of consumption, devouring the limited resources of the earth, and even then requiring continuous renewal of its ephemeral patrimony.

Mechanical work and human work

Another aspect of modern architecture which is difficult to reconcile with the problems of future society—if that society will have the courage to confront the great issue of environmental balance—is the notion that materials are valued according to the amount of work that went into their production. That is, the greatest "status symbol" in architecture, expressing the prestige of the owner or user, is the preciousness or, more accurately, the price of the materials employed. In its tendency toward simplification, toward nudity, modern architecture has stripped form of its symbolic value, transferring that value to materials themselves.

And so decoration has been replaced by bands of shiny marble from far away places, rare metals, soft carpets and fixtures which are expensive, sophisticated and rarely used. A wasteful use of human energy has been replaced by a waste of resources and natural energy. It may be that the latter waste is the more harmful, when one thinks of the plague of unemployment and the difficulty in distributing work between man and the machine in a manner that truly serves the interests of man.

Many myths have been shattered—automation as liberation, the prophecy of a golden age made possible by machines taking over the work of men—and among them are aesthetic myths as well, which had been generated by this hope for a "reign of freedom," exemplified in the automobile.

The analytic emphasis

The dominance of the analytic spirit, and the lack of synthetic vision capable of resolving analyses with integrated decisions rather than unilateral and polemical ones, is another stigma of architecture and planning. It is, in fact, the particular stigma which gave birth to the idea of planning as a separate entity from architecture, creating a false abyss between phenomena which are, in fact, closely interconnected. In ancient civilizations planning came about by means of architecture, with concrete, well defined interventions. Now planning is practiced with large colored charts and endless theorizing, an inevitable "dead letter" method.

It is characteristic for the planner to divide up the land into parts and to establish restrictions, regulations, permanent and transitory norms. The architect arrives later and is faced with a "lot," one of those portions outlined by a colleague's pencil. The architect must then adapt his project to this lot, probably ignoring the adjacent lot which another specialist is working on, isolated in his own little workspace. We know all too well what kind of environmental balance will result. All one needs to do is glance at the urban periphery, and even that is the only area where architecture has dared to break some of its own rules.

If one extends the study of environmental balance to the human sphere, logically taking into account the built environment, one discovers the presence of phenomena which correspond to toxic clouds, and these phenomena have the sad privilege of being permanent. One of the most unbalanced aspects of our new urban environment, (and not only the environment created by speculative building), is the complete disregard for the collective memory of the inhabitants and their notion of space and city. Obviously this doesn't mean an evocation of imitation of the past, but an admission that the past exists in the present and is a crucial part of our environmental balance.

It is certainly too early to predict what exactly post-modern architecture will be or how it will differ from what we are used to. But no one can keep us from hoping that it will be closer to the desires of men and more similar to the descriptions of the prophets of the first industrial revolution, like William Morris, than to those of the second, interrupted revolution who proposed housing units kilometers long, underground cities and mobile homes strung out in rows like drawers in a ghostly steel armature.

What would not be acceptable would be a new architecture created by simply shuffling the cards of the old game, living off a tradition which is already old, although not yet ancient. In any case it is essential to critically review the recent past, courageously weeding out the living from the dead, the branches which still have some life from those which have dried out. This might lead to the toppling of the great prophets—not to deny them their historical due, but to clear the field of many of their proposals which at this point could only be defended by those of macabre tastes.

The modern city, offspring of industrial society in its most mature phase, is the historical embodiment, made tangible, of social alienation. In the modern city the subjugation of man to non-humans ends, contradictory to the real needs of people has assumed extreme and paradoxical forms. The distance between domicile and place of work, the scarcity of social services, pollution, the psychological distance from nature, the molding of relationships according to factory divisions of labor and urban space—all these have created an artificial environment, less favorable than any in history to the establishment of a balanced society or to its orderly development.

During the last century the rising bourgeoisie knew how to give form to a city, for better or worse, according to its own image, and public institutions served to supply the needs of the urban organism. In our century, especially after the second world war, utilitarian and economical alibis have justified the capitalist bourgeoise relegation of new urban construction to the "periphery," winding around the old urban nuclei and destined to assume the role of dormitories, lacking all continuity with the original urban fabric.

The historic urban center and its nineteenth century expansion, through which one still celebrated a rite of "civilized magnificence", have simultaneously become embalmed in their roles as reservoirs of values and symbols which are today only parsimoniously used.

This eclipse of the city, or rather its degradations from complex organism to mere staging ground for artificial consumption, parallels an obsession with privacy in urban life, the eloquent symbols of which are the automobile and the housing blocks of single-family cells, which even resemble in their morphology the walls of funerary niches in great urban graveyards.

Recent decades have seen the emergence of a struggle to claim a new (and in certain ways, ancient) quality of life, often against the background of the alienated urban periphery. There is a recurrent theme of the destruction of privacy as we know it, and the reappropriation of an environment which, working from a participatory base, reconstitutes the framework of collective function which cities in the past offered as a generous gift the largesse of the patron-state.

The revamping of existing cities according to this strategy necessitates a change in direction for traditional planning, which is still grounded in the obsolete dogmas of quantitative criteria and zoning regulations. Such a revision demands a return to direct action, the expression of participatory movements capable of going beyond mere protest. It will also be necessary to acknowledge the great patrimony of specific locales, rediscovering their unmistakable identity, their local realities. Without the renewal of local culture, and the reintegration of a collective consciousness of place, it will be difficult to focus on or find progressive solutions to the fundamental problems of planning which have left their alienating mark on the present urban environment.

The modern city has increasingly ignored the fact that human life is a dependent part of an ecosystem composed of many and diverse forms of life. In its present historic form, the city constitutes an environment no less elusive and misshapen than that of the "countryside," which is really the other side of the urban coin. A reintegration of these two polar models of life implies not only a redistribution of resources, and an abolition of inequitable privilege, but also the development of a new awareness which embodies society's desire to arrest, or at least to slow down, a potentially vertiginous process of impoverishment.

Before architecture can be employed as a tool for intervention through design, it must be used as an investigative tool, looking into the possibilities of new relationships between human habitation and nature. This could be one consequence of our viewing nature as "another form of capital" with which we must pay our bills—not as an infinite source which surrounds us but rather as a "finitude" with which we must establish a new alliance.

If romantic and contemplative naturalism was opposed to the organized rationality of the city and sought the infinitely natural as the site of an interior monologue as evasion of the collective structure today we may look at nature as something society partakes of. Seen in this light, nature must be examined rationally, in order to clearly know the meaning of every human action, especially those actions which have transformed the environment. "The artist is man," Paul Klee has written, "he himself is nature, a fragment of nature within the realm of nature." This dialogue with nature is recognized as a necessary condition of every artistic thought. But until now our culture has paid little heed to this new attitude by which nature removes her hitherto traditional robes of impenetrable mystery isolating her from our perception.

For at least a decade there has been increasing attention paid to ecology. People have become aware that if we don't do something quickly to restore ancient environmental balances which make life possible and often pleasant, for animals and plants as well as human beings, we risk being swept away by a general disorder and chaos from which not even the human race, with its exceptional adaptability, will escape. But a reconciliation with nature is not the only problem facing us if we want to assure our survival and a modicum of continuity with the material and spiritual patrimony that *homo sapiens* has accumulated.

The environment in which man dwells is not just the natural one, but the sum of nature and the built environment: nature transformed by man's work and the goods which form, in their totality, a second nature with its own sense of balance and imbalance. If one thinks about an ecology of man-made environmental balance, developing with equal rigor alongside an ecology of natural environmental balance, it becomes clear that one must react in a global rather than a regional fashion to the problem of survival. One can imagine the construction of a new science of habitation, built on the ruins of the separate disciplines of urban and regional planning, geography and architecture.

FORM FOLLOWS FIASCO

The most insidious (because it is the least predictable) attack on the stagnant orthodoxy of the Modern Movement comes from one of its most brilliant practitioners: Peter Blake, former director of *Architectural Forum* and of *Architecture Plus.* He is also the author, of a successful book, published in 1960, on the holy trinity of modern architecture, Le Corbusier, Mies and Frank Lloyd Wright. This is a work of great conviction, written in a style accessible to a wide audience. In a series of articles published from 1974 on in the magazine, *Atlantic,* Blake faced the themes of obsolescence in the architectural ideas then current. These essays were assembled in book form in 1977 under the unsettling title, *Form Follows Fiasco,* an ironic reworking of the celebrated principle, "form follows function," attributed to Sullivan and universally considered the first commandment of the modern catechism.

This book, as well, was written in a clear, plain style and therefore directed itself to a non-elite audience. It emphasized the fact, underlined in the conclusion, that Blake had been one of the propagandists of the old credo, and moreover that he had practical building experience and, not less importantly, was a user of "modern architecture," having lived and worked in spaces designed by famous architects. The book has the incisive clarity of a pamphlet; of the twelve chapters into which it is divided, eleven are dedicated to as many typical "fantasies" of modern architecture, "fantasies" meaning the guiding ideas, or better, the myths which have animated architectural debate for fifty years.

The first myth Blake analyzes is that of function, posing the question: After so many years of functionalist practice, is it possible to establish whether or not this dogmatic application of a principle has had good results? In other words, does the programming of spaces for specific functions improve the livability of these spaces and their relationship with the user? And what would happen, on the other hand, if these same functions were carried out in buildings which had been destined for other uses? The answer is paradoxical, but forcefully demystifies the axioms which have sustained architecture for many years. Very often the recycling of old buildings for uses entirely different from those for which they were originally intended gives rise to spaces in which the process of adaptation has not only maintained aesthetic levels, but has brought out new potential. Although Blake doesn't emphasize this in his pragmatic approach, one could attribute this stimulating effect to the unleashing of the imagination after years of separation between form and function. The autonomy of formal choices and the correspondence of spaces to a functionalist preconceived model had the effect of cutting off imaginative stimuli and often exercized an authoritative and restraining action on the users, considered as "objects" to be programmed.

Blake's conclusions are implicit in the "historic" examples he cites: the burning by students of the Yale School of Art, a work by Rudolph based on a functional analysis, and the students' request for changes which ignored the architect's spatial designations, the fact that in Great Britain the best concert hall is a recycled brewery (now referred to as "Malting at Snape in Suffolk"); the fact that the best art school in Baltimore is a readapted tram station (the Mont Royal Station, now the Maryland Institute, College of Art); the best library in New York is an adapted courtyard and the best theatre, a transformed library; the most pleasant shopping center in San Francisco (Ghiradelli Square) was once a chocolate factory.

On the one hand Blake disputes that the form of modern architecture truly does follow function, beyond the good intentions of its designer. On the other hand he affirms the relative autonomy and permanence of architectural values with respect to the use of space. Even the distributive flexiblity, proposed by modern architects as a remedy to the varying functional demands of a complex building, is seen by Blake as a sterile myth. Something adapted for any number of uses, he states, risks being an amorphous container. In addition, an adaptability to many functions presupposes extremely costly technical solutions. For example, if one were to build a "total theatre," adapted for every type of production and for a varying number of spectators, the costs would be much greater than those incurred for the construction of a series of individual theatres, appropriate to different types of spectacles and capable of being used all at the same time.

The fantasy of the open plan or "free plan" is compared to the Japanese prototypes from which it is derived. Blake criticizes the open plan for its abstraction which implies a universal solution for spatial problems, a model designed as a response to representative and contemplative demands. In the typical Japanese house the stupendous sequence of spaces, flowing one into the other, separated only by a movable screen, in fact, presupposed a social order based on inequality, where one could count on the presence of numerous servants and where the woman, completely subjugated, had the task of maintaining perfect order in these rooms stripped of furniture, where any element out of place would constitute an unbearable visual disturbance.

Blake takes his cue from this initial observation, commenting with irony on the ominous consequences of the free plan, from the Unite d'Habitation in Marseille to the system now in fashion in modern offices: the so-called "office landscape." He calls the Unite d'Habitation "a formidable cement sculpture," but "as a complex for living, corresponding to the demands of life in the twentieth century, in plan, perspective and in section, and in its spatial organization, it is a farce. Its apartments lack any requisite of privacy; the children's bedrooms are really closets about six feet deep closed by sliding doors; there is no place where the children can get away from the parents, or vice-versa." Masterpieces of virtuoso volumetrics, Le Corbusier's apartments destroy every hypothesis of family life.

As for the "office landscape," where the work space is fitted into open alcoves formed by low pieces of furniture, and light and air from the windows is replaced by fluorescent lights and air conditioning vents, Blake notes that in addition to the waste of space and energy, and given the ominous psychological influence of obligatory promiscuity, the results are tragically deluding. How can it be, he ironically asks, that the architects who invented this absurd system of organization almost always continue to live and work in traditional environments, protected by old walls, illuminated by traditional windows and respectful of true privacy?

The third myth Blake examines is that of purity: supreme aspiration, not only of architecture, but in large part of modern art. This myth has had its most evident expression in the white skins which enclose the volumes of the rationalist factories of the 1920s, recently once again in fashion. These surfaces, sheathed in completely traditional systems, were a response to an intellectual aspiration for a new building material, totally homogeneous and elastic, resistent to inclement weather and to structural settling. Unfortunately this universal material has been neither discovered nor invented, and the abolition of all those traditional architectural elements (cornices, slanted roofs, rain gutters) which were developed specifically in response to a need to employ proven and effective barriers to the ravages of the atmosphere, has rendered most modern buildings impractical over time, or made practical only by very costly finishes and continuous maintenance. If fragility and rapid deterioration are the price to be paid for purity, immediately contaminated by aggressive reality, Blake finds no less serious the tribute paid by modern architecture to the myth of technology and industrialization which for more than a century has forced an unnatural merger between the building industry and industrial production, guided more by the profit motive and a reverence for technology than by rational demands. The greatest industrial power in the world, the United States, where Blake has had practical experience, realizing buildings himself as well as analyzing other people's work, has experimented with every possible system of standardization and prefabrication. And yet the solution to the problems of housing has been sought in the automobile (rather than in housing itself), and the results are, not surprisingly, disappointing.

It would not be feasible to adopt an entirely material approach, which would logically and conveniently entail the serial production of entire buildings by means of industrial systems. Insuperable problems would arise—diversity of climate, varying building codes from region to region, the cost of transportation, the high degree of specialization of labor necessary for assembly. The car and the house, after thirty years of attempting assimilation between the two, making the house a "machine for living," appear as logically and specifically far apart as ever; the methods for manufacturing the one and the other have begun to definitively part ways.

If, then, it is not worth while to aim for greater economy and quality, but, to the contrary, to construct ever more costly buildings and to create unemployment, why do we continue to believe that salvation lies in total industrialization, the panacea for all problems in architecture? Simply because Mies van der Rohe was convinced of this in the 1920s? A typical example of the mistakes which continue to be made in the name of this religious faith in industry is the story of *Habitat* in Montreal, which in fact has provided only negative miracles. Welcomed as an unsurpassable model of residential structure, *Habitat* adapted industrial methods for the production of low cost housing. It was realized at Montreal at a cost which could be justified by its place in the exposition, but an attempt to build a derivative version with the same criteria in Puerto Rico had to be halted in mid-construction due to unresolvable problems of cost and production. The unfinished structure can now be visited as a ruin in flight from technology.

Even the most prestigious product of the technological myth, the skyscraper, is criticized by Blake, with subtle irony, for the effects it has imposed on urban life. He also criticizes the irrational transformations of skyscraper design, from gothic cathedrals in disguise to cellophane packages. The result? . . . alienating rides in elevators, streams of people filing in and out at fixed hours, deserted evenings, streets without daylight and piazzas buffeted by wind which whips along the vertical walls (emitting low sighs, embarrassing all the women) . . . and then there is the madness of walls of glass which produce exaggerated reflections, benefiting only the manufacturers of venetian blinds to shade the windows or the producers of thermal glass to hopefully reduce the useless heat loss of these towers.

Four of the "fantasies" listed by Blake in his critique of the obsolescence of modern theories are dedicated to the city as we know it and have seen it grow under our eyes in the last fifty years, in energetic obedience to the planning principles dedicated to the illusion of creating a more humane habitat. The fantasy of the "ideal city" is dedicated to the great contrasting utopias—Le Corbusier's *Ville Radieuse* and Wright's *Broadacre City*. Le Corbusier, with his *Plan Voisin* and other great projects of the 1920s, predicted a vertical city, made up of isolated skyscrapers standing in large green spaces, traversed by highways. Wright argued for an alternative to the vertical city, where each family would have at its disposal an acre of land to cultivate, a "non-city," made up of single family dwelling harmoniously arranged on an infinite orthogonal grid. Neither the *Ville Radieuse* nor *Broadacre City* were ever built, and the *Plan Voisin*, which Le Corbusier wanted to build in the Marais quarter of Paris, fortunately remained on paper. But, as far as the *Ville Radeuse* is concerned, it makes no sense to argue that this hypothesis for a city cannot be judged since it has not been realized, when the world is now littered with fragments of this utopia, more than sufficient in number to give a clear picture of Le Corbusier's project. As for *Broadacre*, it is in fact an extension of the American suburb, where single family houses extend ad infinitum and the social fabric of the cities is completely destroyed by the great distances.

To demonstrate his theses, Blake gives the example of Zagreb, a city divided into two irreconcilable parts. The old city is swarming with life; the urban scene is animated by the human presence and is in scale with it. The new city consists of vast structures isolated by greenery; the streets are nearly always deserted and there is an absence of places to sit and relax, to meet people, to converse. The radiant city has become, in fact, the geometric city, the city of housing blocks, the city where people don't know each other. The reason people have failed to use this city as intended is obvious: people don't want great deserted spaces, they want things at their own scale, they want to feel themselves among others, like themselves. The best way to achieve this is to have people feel that they are inside something, protected, as if they were in an interior space. The urban alleyways, which Le Corbusier rejected as symbols of bad planning, have proven to be the primary and irreplaceable city factor, the reason that ancient cities are nearly always found to be charming and conducive to social intercourse. The transformation of the street into a highway or a simple communication channel, the transformation of piazzas into indefinite expanses, has robbed the city of its meaning; its continuity has been salvaged only in its historic centers, in America as well, where those centers often date from the 1800s.

The efforts of modern architects to build pieces of authentic cities, to emulate the psychological effects of historic environments, have met with failure. Exceptions can be found, not in the area of "high culture," but in that of popular culture and Kitsch. Disneyland, for example, with its narrow streets, inspired by medieval models, its castles and its little piazzas, is more alive and real, according to Blake, than new Zagreb.

Blake lingers on the aspects of the ideal modern city which are typical and which form its identity: mobility, zoning and housing. The myth that all urban problems can be resolved by rapid transportation- is in direct relationship with the implacable analytic tendency which pushed planners for decades to divide up the city into homogeneous zones according to function: housing, that is, dormitories, in one part; shops in another part, perhaps all joined together in a shopping center; in still another part, offices; and in another, places of entertainment; beyond, on the edges of the countryside, sports and manufacturing installations. To this waste of mechanical energy caused by the necessity to be continually on the move, one can add the waste of human energy. Hundreds of hours are spent by people waiting for a green light or scurrying across gasoline-stained streets.

If ancient cities were a continuum in which the most diverse functions were interwoven, creating ever-present psychological stimuli for the inhabitants, as well as conditions conducive to encounters and socializing, then modern cities, especially those where architects have made their presence felt, have become images of schizophrenia and living examples of waste. On the one hand there are the business centers, deserted in the evening and on weekends, convulsively overpopulated during work hours. On the other hand there is the periphery, abandoned during work hours and invaded by streams of irritable people during rush hour. And yet planning theories maintain that this division into ghettos and imposition of order should help people and better their lives.

The problem of mass housing has engendered the most profound and paradoxical application of the zoning principle. Preoccupations with "hygiene" have led to streets enlarged to the point of becoming squalid spaces without dimension. The abstract assignation of public land to areas of separation between housing blocks has placed enormous distances between people, substituting the continuous fabric of the city with the chaos of the dormitory-periphery, where buildings are arranged like pawns on a chessboard, according to a logic incomprehensible to its inhabitants.

According to Blake housing blocks were built after the industrial revolution in the service of speculation, government and bureaucracy. One might add that they demonstrate the degree to which those three powers, in alliance, have distanced man from his own goals and desires.

The last myth examined is that of design and its effects on interior furnishings. Blake entitles this chapter, *The Fantasy of Form,* and with great irony reviews the achievements of the avant-garde in this area. Armchairs such as Rietveld's "red-blue" "cannot be abandoned without the help of an orthopedic surgeon." Chairs like Rietveld's "Berlin-chair" would seem to justify their assymmetry by a presupposition that there have been profound genetic mutations in the human race. Pieces of furniture such as those designed by Le Corbusier, Mies van der Rohe and Breuer, which certainly correspond perfectly to the need to keep living spaces fluid and transparent, nonetheless, with their hard materials, square shapes and theoretical responses to the movements of the body, fail to perform their primary function and remain above all magnificent sculptures to admire. Blake concludes that the modern masters used to say, "We reject the tyranny of form."

Content—or 'problem solving'—was the name of their game. Quite so; but the problem that the Modern Movement really wants to solve, judging by its performance to date, is the infuriating anatomy of the human race: nothing, dammit, is going to function—Bauhauswise—unless all men are redesigned as cubes, and all women redesigned as spheres. Once that is accomplished, everything else will fall into place with a barely audible click—and the solution will then become the problem.

The conclusions of Blake's book acquire the solemn character of a request, above all to architects, for a "moratorium," through which their products would cease furnishing lessons and would agree to "serve" men.

So the post-modern world is here, whether we like it or not. It was not invented by revisionist critics. It was spawned by the modern masters themselves, and by many of their failures. And now, what are the alternatives?

The first alternative to the modern dogma is a moratorium on high-rise construction, an abandonement of the myth of the super-skyscraper, the negative consequences of which to the well being of the city are by now evident and which could become even more dramatic in the future. The second moratorium deals with the destruction of existing buildings, whether or not they hold historic interest. The politics of the destruction and rebuilding of parts of the city is nonsensical in a world which must utilize all its resources to face the problem of demographic growth and which can longer examine problems of the economy in terms favorable to avarice and cupidity.

The third alternative to the modern dogma is the interruption of construction of super-highways which, in already developed nations, has produced a series of phenomena twisting around the urban organism and have become symbols of a gigantic and useless waste of fuel, cement, metal, tar and human time.

Blake's fourth alternative is legislative reform with regard to construction materials, which would hold manufacturers responsible for the performance of their products. The use of untested materials, and their imposition through advertising which stresses the worth of anything new, endangers not only the solidarity and durability of our buildings, but, in very direct and dramatic fashion, our safety as well. In fact, there is no lack of cases of poisoning linked to wide spread use of new substances. (Blake cites the example of an acoustical insulation used in the construction of the School of Art and Architecture at Yale University, later found to be highly carcinogenic.) The fire which destroyed within minutes the hugh Buckminister Fuller sphere, built for the World's Fair in Montreal, acquired an especially sinister symbolism. Fortunately the fire occurred after the closing of the Fair; otherwise, ten thousand people could have been buried beneath a stream of incandescent plastic.

The fifth alternative is a moratorium on monofunctional zoning which has divided the city into ghettos, destroying the vital mix of differentiated activities.

"Isfahan," writes Blake, "the most marvelous of all cities, has never heard of zoning; its inhabitants work where they live, do their shopping where they work, pray where they play and socialize where they work. Monofunctional zoning—a notion advanced very seriously by the Modern

Movement—signifies very simply the end of urban civilization."

The new approach which derives from an abandonment of the zoning is hinted at in Blake's sixth alternative which proposes planning on a human scale, with modest but concrete objectives in terms which are comprehensible to and controlled by everyone, making possible participatory process. This is the philosophy stated by Schumaker in his adage, "small is beautiful," an antidote to totalitariam immensity and planning in the style of Haussmann and Speer which has so often exercised a perverse fascination for modern planners and architects.

Blake's seventh alternative is a radical transformation of architectural education which is currently oriented toward the production of generalists rather than specialists in design and construction. The last and eighth alternative is a moratorium on architecture itself, that is a refusal to further enrich the ideal museum of masterpieces, which modern architecture has certainly helped to fill, paying the price, however, of a growing distance between what the experts call architecture and the desires, the needs, the aspirations of the people.

Blake concludes:

It has truly been a fantastic period in the history of architecture in more ways than one. Affirming its faith in reason, the Movement was in fact the most irrational occurence since the sweet madness of Ludwig of Bavaria. Affirming its faith in the common man and an egalitarian world, it stirred up people on both the right and the left, in the service of either private enterprise or the State. Affirming its total devotion to technology, it betrayed methods and materials of construction with the lightheartedness of a circus clown. Affirming its dedication to the idea of city as the unique wellspring of civilization, it rendered the city ungovernable and in effect scattered its inhabitants to the wind. No period in the history of architecture has been more creative or more destructive or more oppressive, both for architects and for innocent spectators.

The book's conclusions are neither optimistic nor catastrophic. Blake observes that the moratorium on modern architecture has already begun, with the initiative of architects themselves, divided into two camps: at one extreme are the designers of non-buildable buildings; at the other the designers of buildable non-buildings, realizable structures which are not buildings in an architectural sense.

THE PRIMITIVES OF A NEW SENSIBILITY

It is useless to turn away from the past to think only of the present. It is a dangerous illusion to even think that this would be possible. An opposition between present and past is absurd. The future doesn't bring us anything, doesn't give us anything; it is for us to build it, we must give ourselves to it, even give our lives. But to give, it is necessary to possess, and we possess no other life, no other lymph, than the treasures inherited from the past, and digested, assimilated, recreated by us. Among all the needs of the human soul none is more vital than the past.

SIMONE WEIL, *L'Enracinement*, Gallimard, Paris, 1949

As with all the alternating movements and styles of past centuries, the "modern"—(that repertory of forms which, after a creative incubation during the early decades of this century, took shape in Europe and in America during the 1930s and spread rapidly throughout the world)—also is destined, beyond its dawn and its full day, to an inevitable sunset. In *The Language of Post-Modern Architecture*, (Academy Editions, London, 1977), Charles Jencks, a brilliant Anglo-Saxon scholar who has analyzed the most recent developments in architecture from a linguistic point of view, believes that this sunset has already occurred. With lucid irony he pinpoints the exact date for the death of "modern architecture": he has it coincide—at 3:32 PM, July 15, 1972—with the dynamiting of the Pruitt-Igoe housing project, which had been build in 1951 according the "the most progressive ideals of CIAM" (the international organization of modern architects created by Le Corbusier in 1928 at La Sarraz castle) and had

been given an award by the American Institute of Architecture.

This neighborhood was provided with public parks, pedestrian paths and community services. It was planned according to the prescribed standards of modern urban science, with large beehive buildings eleven stories high, endless corridors and immense, repetitive architectural spaces. It became a sort of prison for the inhabitants, and at the same time a tangible symbol of their exploited condition. This identification between architecture and the quality of urban life caused a hostile reaction among the inhabitants, the majority of whom were black, which found expression in violence and vandalism.

The possibility of restoring or readapting the project for other use was dismissed by psychologists and sociologists who held the architecture itself in large part responsible for this pathological phenomenon. It isn't surprising, when one thinks that for some time now a phrase has been used to described a growing social malady—"balcony syndrome"—the morbid consequences of oppressive social control, occuring in certain building types which modern architects continue to consider optimum.

Jenck's strongest charge against "modern architecture" is its intellectual and abstract character, which has led to its rapid obsolescence. It is based on axioms which have never been proven and have never confronted the real needs of men. It came into being, like a custom-made suit, for a mythical modern man who existed only in the minds of the architects and who bore increasingly little resemblance to flesh and blood citizens. The quantitative and exaggeratedly analytical approach to the problems of *Habitat*, for example, took very little note of the breakdown caused by the enormous increase in sheer numbers, of things and people brought together. People seem to have lost the ability to judge "how big is too big," and the consequences can be seen in the modern day metropolis, with its houses and office buildings the size of pyramids. (In Rome, for example, there is a kilometer long housing project under construction at Corviale).

Another charge made by Jencks is the reductive nature of modern architecture: its unwavering concern with pared down, increasingly sterile content; its fascination with the rationality of the machine and industrial production; environmental hygiene; purity raised to a supreme value. All this has produced something similar to what Pasolini called "homologation," seen in the transparency and repetitiveness of an office building, the ubiquitous whiteness of a hospital, the rigid organization of a factory. These are the dominant characteristics of the city, which has become an undifferentiated factory city, bureaucracy city, hospital city, pro-ducing an equivalent monotony in both places of work and residence, in both public and collective spaces.

The myth of social reform was the ideal element which originally justified and even saw as heroic the reductiveness of the language of modern architecture. According to Le Corbusier, society could hopefully be changed through architecture, thereby avoiding political revolution. Both the myth and the hopes having been shattered, what sense can there be to such architectural "univalence"? According to Jencks it is high time to change direction. Actually, Jencks says, it is about time we noticed that a new wave of architects, those who first saw, or better, understood, the needs of our time, has already changed direction. For nearly twenty years they have fought their battle as a minority and they foreshadow the main line of a different type of architecture, one which once again embraces history.

One can pick out the characteristics of this Post-Modern architecture above all by comparing it with the tradition of the Modern Movement, but also by making analogies with the cultural production of periods historically similar to our own, such as Mannerism and the Baroque. First of all, Post-Modern architecture is evolutionary more than revolutionary. It doesn't negate the modern tradition, but freely interprets it, integrates it, critically reviews it for its glories and its errors. It reacts against dogmas of reduction, personal style, static or dynamic equilibrium, purity and the absence of every "vulgar" element. Post-Modern architecture reevaluates ambiguity and irony, plurality of styles, double standards which allow for popular taste on the one hand, through historic or vernacular references, and on the other hand provide issues of specific interest for the practitioner (explication of working processes, a "chess game" approach to the composition and decomposition of the architectural object).

The new tendency has reacted to modern architecture's dogmatic, inhibited distance from history which denied it the main tool of popular understanding, that is, collective memory. Post-Modern architecture upholds the necessity of interaction between historical memories and new traditions, and above all the "recontextualization" of architecture, the establishment of a precise relationship, or a dialectical nature, between new buildings and the environment which sustains it, be it the urban periphery or the historic center.

An ironic posture, tolerant and inexhaustibly curious about what already exists, has taken the place of the prophetic, severe and prescriptive posture of the masters of the Modern Movement and, even more so, their followers. Robert Venturi, one of the first practitioners of this new line, and the author of what Jencks calls the first Post-Modern anti-monument, studied the urban environment of Las Vegas with the same philological rigor with which Letarouilly inventoried the Roman Renaissance. After Venturi a whole group of architects have dedicated entire analyses to existing examples of architectural vernacular and, above all, those of the last fifty years. They have paid special attention to modifications made to houses by proprietors and tenants, that is, a phenomenon where it is possible to deduce an active and concrete relationship between the users of architecture and the architectural products which form a part of their daily lives.

This renewed attention to architecture as a collective product comes out of a rather profound understanding of the urban phenomenon. It is a line of study which, after a long period of silence, restores "the word" to architecture, through the reappropriation of metaphor and symbol and the capacity of shape itself to evoke not just abstract ideas, but also forms which accord with the taste and sensibility of the people. This new tendency also allows architecture to criticize and dissent as well as accept, always, however, from the vantage of widely accepted and understood standards.

The exponents of Post-Modernism are singled out by Jencks, not as intentional adherents to an organized movement, but as creators of a new climate and participants, despite their divergent personal orientations, in a new emerging wave. Alongside Venturi and Charles Moore, Robert Stern, Stanley Tigerman and Thomas Gordon Smith, Jencks places architects such as Lucien Kroll, Ralph Erskine, Peter Eisenman, Lluis Clotet and Oscar Tusquets, Andrew Derbyshire, Aldo van Eyck and Theo Bosch. This is a grouping of architects which heralds a widening of horizons; their works can be read as symptoms, hints of a transformation which will have the 1980s as its field of action.

Jencks writes:

We may expect to see the next generation of architects using the new hybrid language with confidence. It will look more like Art Nouveau than the International Style, incorporating the rich frame of reference of the former, its wide metaphorical reach, its written signs and vulgarity, its symbolic signs and cliches—the full gamut of architectural expression." The present architects are "the primitives of a new sensibility.

THE STAR SYSTEM
AND THE CRISIS OF THE
FUNCTIONALIST STATUTE

The "functionalist statute" had barely been articulated, toward the end of the 1920s, when a strong reactionary shift seemed to threaten its achievement, at least in some of the countries where it had taken root. The spread of Fascism in Europe in the 1930s, the political crises of the democratic regimes following the crash of '29 and the turning inward of the Soviet Union after Lenin's death, in fact, partially truncated the growing influence of the new architecture. These events also put an end to an illusion harbored by a good number of intellectuals—that their ideas would be officially taken up by the Soviet Union, the only modern state born out of the socialization of the means of production.

The turn of events was no less dramatic in the Weimar Republic, crucible of the most advanced ideas of the time and a testing ground for a welding together of the new architecture and social-democratic reform. In the wake of the Nazi's rise to power, modern architecture was demoted to the category of "degenerate art," and the new regime retained from it only those aspects which they deemed compatible with its ideological pro-gram.

Even in the Western democracies, the function-alist statute was accepted with some suspicion, and its application was limited to building, both public and private, which by its very nature did not challenge the status quo.

Seeing it in perspective, however, one could say that while political difficulties—above all the rejection of modernism by the most reactionary regimes—may have slowed down the spread of modern architecture, these very difficulties also helped along its cause. When the world emerged from the nightmare of World War II, it rediscovered modern architecture as a symbol of progress, parallel to democracy itself, as well as to technology and industry; in these ideals rested the hopes of mankind.

Modern architecture was put to the test in terms of the great tasks of reconstruction and productive reorganization, albeit in a limited manner from the technological and economic point of view. But even with severe limitations, architects were given the chance to realize their ideal models, and above all, the entire world was made available to the pursuit of internationalism. Any doubts about the new aesthetic's capacity to accomplish its mission vanished with the collapse of the myths and sym-bols of the old regime. The lack of symbols of power other than economic values and production efficiency corresponded perfectly to the new con-cept of "state" in the most developed industrialized countries, where economic and political power no longer needed to distinguish their spheres of action.

In this way, after the war, the functionalist statute took hold and spread until the 1960's, in a euphoric climate of aggressive economic and bureaucratic power. Modern architecture, in its mature style in the 1930s, had been able to assume a diaphanous elegance, the style of the most refined upper middle class, without ostentation. In the postwar period, however, it had to hurriedly reclothe itself in the vulgar and coarse manner of the nouveau riche, in the vanguard of the economic boom and the unbridled building speculation.

The crisis of the Modern Movement, however, really began before the misleading triumph of the functionalist statute. From 1880 until 1910, during its contentious infancy, the Modern Movement was a culture in crisis, maintaining a pluralistic character, a totality of discordant attempts without a definable objective in terms of its language. Its crisis was that of the bourgeoisie faced with the failure of their ideals following their rise to power, a crisis of society as a whole, subject through the generalization of industrial productive processes to a radical upheaval without historic precedent, and without any ultimate regulation. The pioneers of the Modern Movement saw this society as the victim of a machine gone mad, the mechanisms of which needed to be brought back under control.

It is only after the interval of the First World War and the early post-war period, symbolized by the romantic utopia of the Expressionists, that the Modern Movement took on a triumphant air, giving itself a historically palingenetic and steadying function. "Architecture instead of (and to avoid and take the place of) Revolution," states Le Corbusier; "architecture to bring about justice and equality," state the rationalists; "architecture to express and exalt the 'spirit of the time,'" the zeitgeist.

According to Gropius, the new architecture is not a new style but a victory over every possible style; technical and aesthetic processes are self evident, safeguarding architectural investigations from every deviation and error: the correct construction, the architectural act which is at one with the productive system is worthwhile in and of itself and has absolute quality. This metaphysical ideology of architecture as "truth" allows the functionalist statute to make its case amidst historic difficulties of every type, during one of the most dramatic periods in the history of the world. Meanwhile the Fascist dictatorships were unleashing their irrational power, and a war of unforseeable dimensions shattered the precarious political balances of the entire world. The promise of absolute rationality and of a permanent and rigid link with industrial development made the white volumetric architecture of the rationalist masters seem to be the "substance of things apart," the symbol of a desparate appeal for a world restored to reason and brotherhood.

In America, after the crash of 1929, the International Style supplanted the symbolic modernism of the New York school which has created a language of fascinating complexity for the last heroic phase of confident capitalism. This very supplanting became, in its turn, a "style," counter to Gropiusian intentions, a repertory of forms and meanings immediately taken up by high financial circles for its "noble" promise of austerity. This austerity was meant for everyone and was seen as necessary for the consecration of a new alliance with the working class, under the banner of industrial patriotism.

This patrimony of reassuring certainties—sufficiently ambiguous to lead to equivocal agreements and alliances—was challenged, even before the war, by two masters, Aalto and Wright. They called for "the pleasure of architecture" and the necessity for poetic license, but their heresy was tolerated as a marginal deviation. Such was the power of the historians that they were able to incorporate Aalto and Wright into their grand scheme, as "exceptions which prove the rule." In the post-war period, widely read works such as Giedion's *Space, Time and Architecture* and Zevi's *History of Modern Architecture* presented modern architecture as a veritable "star system," in which recognized masters exchange well determined but, in the long run, interchangeable roles and offer linguistic repertories from which one can choose or mix together.

For years there was a dilemma among lesser architects, but by no means restricted to them— "Wright or Le Corbusier?"—a dilemma endowed with all the petty rivalry and jealousies of a soccer match.

As early as the 1950s, the two spirits of the Modern Movement, the prophetic and believing and the analytic and reflective, which had been temporarily forced to co-exist, began to disagree. A full-scale rupture, however, was averted. The first evidence of a fracture comes from the masters themselves, tired of reciting the role assigned to them by historians which, relegating them into symbols, had removed them from the vicissitudes of the human condition. Le Corbusier stupified his followers, molding the Ronchamps chapel on the top of a hillside in southeastern France, where he seemed to attempt to free himself from that enlightened secularism which was inseparable from his image. Wright created a scandal by citing Sullivan in the facade of a flower store in San Fran-cisco, but even more so by incorporating columns and cubic capitals in his Baghdad project. Gropius designed the American Embassy in Athens with the explicit inspiration of the ruins of the Parthenon.

During the 1930s, Jacobus Pieter Oud had been the object of severe reprimands for having proposed a "too pleasant" building for Shell, in which timid decorations appeared—an example of deviationism similar to those celebrated during those years by the Marxist orthodoxy. During the 1950s the debate took other turns, more compliant and less rigorous, although the continuity of development of the Modern Movement was never seriously called into question.

Reviewing the critical and above all the architectural output from a distance of over twenty years, certain things become clear. The orthodoxy of the functionalist statute cracked and crumbled when faced with the great theme of its relationship with history and with collective memory. The masters were the most broadminded about reaching for this forbidden fruit, in their reproposing an involvement with memory, which they themselves had intentionally interrupted. Le Corbusier, in La Tourette, transcribed the spatial structure of the convent of Le Thoronnet, evoking the magic of its contrasts of light and shade. At Chandigarh he took the sequence of the large arches from the baths of Rome and the intersections from Michelango's Campidoglio. Wright amused himself by taking apart his own image which had been divided up into periods by the historians. He ran backwards and forwards within his own biography, taking from his personal styles as well as their historic inspirations, from Japanese to Mayan civilization. In some works, based on the theme of the circle, he more or less intentionally made reference to baroque spatial studies. The next generation, as well, lost their timidity and ventured a return to expressiveness and symbolism. Saarinen and Tange, in some of their most exemplary works, went back to modelling structural forms with expressionistic nostalgia. Eero Saarinen's chapel at M.I.T. in Cambridge, Massachusetts (1950-55) reappropriates masonry technology and a theatrical device for illumination and a materialization of rays of light which derives from Bernini's Cornaro chapel.

Philip Johnson, who is today unanimously considered the patriarch of Post-Modernism, played a fundamental role in this detachment from modernist orthodoxy. Together with Russell Hitchcock, Johnson had coined the formula of the International Style in 1932, recognizing the stylistic, and therefore relative and transient, nature of the language elaborated by the European masters of functionalism. Collaborating with Mies van der Rohe in the realization of the Seagram's Building, he had played a part in the definition of one of the undisputed masterpieces of the most orthodox modern architecture. These circumstances emphasize and give particular meaning to his courageous declaration with which, at the beginning of the 1960s, he decreed the "end of modern architecture."

Writing to Jurgen Joedicke in 1961, after having read his *History of Modern Architecture*, Johnson expressed himself as follows:

There is only one absolute thing today, and it is change. There are no rules, absolutely no given truths in any of the arts. There is only the sensation of a marvelous freedom, of an unlimited possibility to explore, of an unlimited past of great examples of architecture from history to enjoy.

I am not worried about a new eclecticism. Even Richardson, who considered himself an eclectic, was not one at all. A good architect will always do original work. A bad architect would do the worst "modern" work, just as he would do the worst work (that is, imitations) with historical forms.

Structural honesty for me is one of those infantile nightmares from which we will have to free ourselves as soon as possible·...

I am old enough to have immensely enjoyed the international style and to have worked within its limits with great joy. I still believe that Le Corbusier and Mies are the greatest living architects. But now the epoch changes so quickly. Old values spread again with vertiginous yet electrifying speed. Long live Change!

The danger that you see of a sterile, academic eclecticism is not a danger. The danger is in the opposite, in the sterility of your Academy of the modern movement.

Prophetic words which already sense the risk of sterility inherent in efforts to artificially sustain a "movement," transformed into a static series of conventions. In his architecture Johnson responds to the new situation and follows with detachment, as an impartial witness, first the uncertain and mannered historicism of Yamasaki, Stone and Johnson, then the great parabola of Kahn and the work of his disciples, Venturi and Moore and the New York Five. Each one of his latest skyscrapers is a point of resolution of a continuous oscillation, a testimonial to a strategy which is opposed to every return to the "ranks," even those of Post-Modernism. His attitude is that of the "wiseman," ready to protect every new anticonformist attempt but determined to remain uninvolved in new myths and new illusions.

ITALY IN RETREAT

The developments which deviate most explicitly from modern orthodoxy unexpectedly occur in Italy. Historic events placed Italian architecture at the center of critical attention in the late 1940s. Italy was finally free from Facism, which had strongly influenced the development of the rationalist movement, first advocating it and then restricting it to compromise and surrender, and so it was thought that it would be an ideal place for nurturing an ordered, obedient development of the most general hypotheses of the European Modern Movement. The architectural world in England, through the pages of *Architectural Review*, the most influential European Journal during those years, on many occasions clearly expressed this anticipation and hope. The earliest products of the Italian reconstruction, which began laboriously between 1947 and 1950, (notably late, considering the political and economic difficulties in which the country found itself), were greeted with curiosity and pleasure.

This early enthusiasm made the subsequent delusion all the more scathing, as can be seen in the violent criticism unleashed by Rayner Banham in 1957, in the pages of the same *Architectural Review*, where he spoke explicitly of the "retreat of Italy from the vanguard of the Modern Movement" and the "infantile regression" of Italian architecture. The attack is probably unique from a historical point of view and perfectly expresses the intolerant and dogmatic climate of the militant criticism of the Modern Movement. The condemnation, expressed with the harshness of a court of Inquisition, assails the cultural bent of an entire nation on the basis of a single fault: that of having distanced itself from the accepted truths of the modern tradition.

What exactly was happening of so controversial and vital a nature in Italy during the early 1950s? A young scholar, wanting to understand the issues in detail, would have been able to read the magazines and newspapers of the time, and could have studied the archives and the ongoing architectural debates, much as one would a mystery story, seeking to unravel the thread of a crime. None of the historians who were concerned with contemporary architecture thought it opportune to carefully look into this state of events, partially because the very point of view which might have helped them to understand what was happening—namely an "exit from the Modern Movement"—was still untested. Nonetheless there were developments of great significance, demonstrated by the conflicts which emerged between critics and theoreticians on one hand and architects on the other. As is often the case, the critics were behind the times in terms of architectural practice, and if they were rarely stimulating, they were terribly strong in their repression of new ideas and their pleas for order.

Our objective here is not to reconstruct these developments in detail, but to attempt to connect them in an overall plan, and we will limit ourselves to the recounting of certain particularly significant episodes in Italy. With this end in mind, it is especially useful to review the various camps in order to study the relationships and movements between them, thereby distinguishing two cultural centers, Rome and Milan, which present only apparently analogous sides.

The "academics" played a passive but influential role, especially in terms of professional power. This group was made up of the architects who had willingly adapted to the standards of Facism and had maintained positions of power, both in the university and in the non-academic world. There were some talented architects among them—Piacentini, Del Debbio and Foschini in Rome; Muzio and Portaluppi in Milan. All of them, however, with the exception of Muzio, became virtual agents of the regime, and the price they paid was a progressive and ineluctable loss of true creative passion or personal direction.

The group of "rationalists," under the leadership of Pagano, director of *Casabella*, confronted the academics head on at the beginning, but they, too, became more accomodating and oblique in their criticism. The deaths of Pagano, who had opened his eyes to the realities of Fascism only during the war, and of Terragni, the most talented and coherent member of the younger generation, left the rationalist camp substantially leaderless. There were also tremendous feelings of guilt, for concessions made to regressive Fascist tastes, especially after the Nazi influence from 1937 on. This regression was indelibly expressed in the marble and travertine of E42, the new center of Rome (later called EUR), hastily topped with arches and columns under the guidance of Piacentini.

The rationalists felt these losses, but their ranks were replenished by the new generation, whose center was Milan, where they formed the *MSA*. This group took as its mission the salvation and development of the architectural inheritance from the 1930s. Another, alternative choice was offered by a group centered in Rome, the Association for Organic Architecture. Among the active partici-pants of that group was Bruno Zevi, who had been an architecture student in Rome during the dark pre-war period and who had gone underground during the racial persecutions of the Fascist regime. Zevi had made a fruitful visit to America, during which he had studied with Gropius and had been initiated into the Frank Lloyd Wright cult. The APAO (Association for Organic Architecture) raised the Wrightian banner of organic architecture and often cloaked itself in the prophetic and op-timistic aura of the American pioneer, to the extent of allowing its members to sign a sort of oath, reminiscent of the Mazzinian "Young Italy."

Zevi's work was first seen in the severely analytic design of the early issues of *Metron*. He then expressed himself through a pamphlet which in its title made reference to Le Corbusier's most well know theoretical work, *Toward an Architec-ture*. Zevi's *Toward an Organic Architecture*, (which presages his *History of Modern Architec-ture*, written some years later), presents itself as a catalyst for a tendency, inspired as much by Wright's fragile theoretical formulations as by his actual architecture. This tendency was seen as a victory over, rather than an alternative to, rationalism, which Zevi branded with the derisive epithet "rationalist squarings."

The relationship among these three forces—the academics, the rationalists and the organicists—determined, during the first fifteen years of the post-war period, a series of calculated moves, like a chess match, without any conclusive outcome, but only demonstrated the ability of any one side to neutralize the others. The academics firmly held on to their positions of power in the universities and the institutions, but they accepted as vic-torious an acritical and pluralist version of the hypotheses of the Modern Movement. The rationalists opposed the "Americanizing" tendencies of the organicists, but they gradually absorbed them, claiming the necessity for self-criticism from within their own ranks. (This had first seen its culmination in Pagano's rediscovery of the peasant tradition in the exhibition organized by the 1936 Triennial.) The organicists, for their part, saw their polemic strength and internal cohesion rapidly corroded.

Zevi's aggressiveness and conviction did not find an outlet in architectural works capable of establishing new guidelines. His group's early efforts produced little that was new—an occasional inclined surface, some acute or obtuse angles—the prevailing flat building morphology which had resulted from a corruption of the rationalist vocabulary. Zevi was wary of any imitation of the extremely personal, and therefore unrepeatable, language of Wright, but translating verbal formulas into architecture has always been difficult. The actual production of the organicists, indicated in Zevi's *History of Modern Architecture* of 1953—a restaurant in Sabaudia, a few mediocre houses which today are difficult to distinguish from the surrounding squalor of the urban periphery—convey a surprising sense of failure.

The disbanding of APAO and the crisis of MSA ended any thoughts of reuniting the most active groups, and a new period of practical experimentation began. Certain architects emerged on the scene—Albini, Gardella, the BBPR group, Michelucci, Ridolfi, Scarpa—each in autonomous fashion, and demonstrating personal, almost intimate, points of view. They made a fundamental contribution to the definition of an "Italian line," the significance of which one can perhaps only appreciate today, in the face of the "post-modern" tendency. The young generation of architects just out of school gave new life to this movement, especially around Padua, banding together to articulate a new style, the Neo-Liberty, which was dismissed by others with summary intolerance.

The theme of memory emerged in the work of the Italian masters during the early years of reconstruction, and the first images were tied to an old passion, cultivated by Pagano, for the models of peasant culture. Gardella's house for a vineyard owner in 1945, Ridolfi's farm projects (1946) and Michelucci's church in Collina (1946) are three different echoes, all made possible by the rationalist experience. Three convergent works by three different personalities: Gardella, critic within the rationalist system, possessed a personal orientation which allowed him to insert humble materials and eloquent elements of the artisan tradition into an otherwise elegant, geometric fabric. Ridolfi, after an academic apprenticeship, colored, however, by a dose of metaphysics and the Neo-Baroque which nurtured expressionistic values (during a significant term of study in Germany), had built a house in Rome according to Loosian standards, at the beginning of the war. Michelucci realized the most valid and esteemed example of monumental building before the war with his station in Florence, and he had accomplished this with a vocabulary extraneous to the asceticism of the International Style. He used glass in expressive and symbolic terms which recalled developments in Germany, more than Le Corbusier's planes of glass. In Michelucci's work an adhesion to regionalism was further emphasized by a strong tie to Tuscany and his architectural experiences there, and by an extremely direct and binding relationship with the academics, a relationship which had led to projects of a distinctly provincial nature during the war years.

The convergence of three such different personalities on the theme of memory during the early post-war years demonstrates the existence of a cultural propensity easily comprehensible in a country constrained to a rapid descent from the false pride and megalomaniacal plans of provincial imperialism, and a latecomer to the dramatic struggle for survival. It is easy to recognize in these images the same ferment which paused directors like Rossellini, De Sica and Visconti toward cinematographic "neo-realism." The dates on record confirm a parallel development between architecture and cinema; the period of incubation for both fields, before the war, also coincides, a period which prepared the ground for the innovative works which followed.

There is no critical basis for the thesis that these developments were the result of concessions made to the academics, and therefore a direct consequence of anti-modern polemics, introduced in the late 1930s under the influence of Hitlerian Neo-Classicism, and this is in contrast with the given facts. The orientation of the academics, who had never been open to the idea of vernacular, in reality advocated a form of internationalism, disconnected from its environmental context, and following the war, a sort of guild complex resulted in the acritical acceptance of the most neutral professional standards.

Anyone who studied at the universities during those years when the old academics were in power can testify to the suspicion which greeted the idea of a "recourse to memory," in the manner proposed by Ridolfi, Gardella and Albini. Their ideas were interpreted almost as a regression and a revenge on the part of problem students. One of the jurors for the competition for the Rome station, for example, who himself had constructed buildings in pure "Mussolinian" style, acted decisively to prevent the prize from going to the Ridolfi-Quaroni group, stating that their project, with its vaulted ceilings, had been inspired by the nearby Baths of Diocletian. For years this very juror had drawn from history in a mechanical and reductive manner, based on the simplification and "stylization" of models of nineteenth century derivation. And yet to him, this resort to memory, delicately wrought with subtle allusions, which attempted to reawaken familiar structures and etymologies within the realm of the collective memory, appeared to be incomprehensible intellectualizing, as, in indeed, rationalism had appeared ten years earlier.

One can understand the lack of communication if one stops to think that those academics had been bound to their imperial evocations with the same spirit with which they surrendered to the neutral technology of the International Style, at the demise of Fascism. In both cases their choice was for an architecture of consensus. On the other hand, in searching out historical and environmental roots, the most senstive architects affirmed their dissent from the obligatory path of the by now gratuitous and unproductive triumph of modernist orthodoxy.

To what extent did these convergent efforts of the exponents of what we can now define as the "Italian School" anticipate and prefigure a departure from the Modern Movement, allowing, twenty years later, the identification of a Post-Modern movement? Charles Jencks, as we have already noted, was the first historian to confront this issue in systematic fashion, and he has recognized a prescient role in these Italian investigations. But he places them in his "Evolutionary Tree" under the label Neo-Liberty. Even before the Neo-Liberty movement was born, there was a great deal of architectural activity which can be discussed using the very categories outlined in Jencks' book, such as contextualism, the return to decoration and eclectic historicism.

With regard to contextualism, works such as Michelucci's Commodities Exchange, the first version of Gardella's Venetian House in Zattere and Ridolfi and Quaroni's project for the Rome station are all symptomatic examples of a mirroring of environmental data, translated into a conscious mix with traditional vocabulary and modern methods and elements. The objective is neither pastiche nor revival, but environmental harmony.

Contextualization, and, therefore, the investigation of a dialogue among diverse elements and a consonance-dissonance with the surroundings, immediately tends to expand to an understanding of the "historic" presence which goes beyond mere material juxtaposition of the old and the new. This can be seen in works like the Veritti house by Scarpa, steeped in Venetian memories, or the houses by Gardella and Albini in the Mangiagalli quarter of Milan, or Ridolfi's Ina houses in Cerignola and Treviso. These are neo-vernacular statements of great maturity, and together they work to gather up primordial memories to create a new atmosphere, as in Albini's treasury of San Lorenzo, inspired by the morphology of ancient villages, where the functionalist impetus is overwhelmed by the strong, evocative potential of the designed forms.

The eclectic approach can also be seen in the abandonment of the autobiographical nature of the coherent personal style demanded by the "star-system" of the 1930s. Diverse expressions are tied more to place than to the development of personal hypotheses.

The Italian contribution to the rediscovery of decoration is no less significant. Ridolfi's houses along the Viale Etiopia, masterpieces of architectural neo-realism, reintroduced, in the window sills, decorative elements inspired by the carpets which used to be hung outside windows during religious and civil ceremonies. (Ridolfi claims to have taken the idea from an eighteenth century house by Marino in which the improvised draperies appear to be "congealed" in the stucco.) Luigi Moretti, another talented exponent of this school of "evoked memory", employed the use of rustication in a building in the Girasole section of Rome, where a vibrating play of light and shadow gives the feeling of a virgin material, juxtaposed to the pure volumes in the rationalist tradition. In a house in San Marinella he brought back the use of molding, in the horizontal striations of the cylindrical volume which emerge from beneath a rough covering of plaster. Moretti is also responsible for a theoretical proposition, both provocative and stimulating, calling for an interpretation of ancient monuments based on the transformation of internal spaces into volumes. This interpretation stripped these symbols of the past of their literal meaning, making it possible to use them in autonomous fashion, for their formal qualities—an approach also taken by Louis Kahn.

We have already seen that the work of this Italian school did not meet with a warm critical reception. Even Bruno Zevi, who had himself pointed out the obsolescence of the functionalist dogmas, was cautiously negative, then openly hostile to Mario Ridolfi's neo-realist solutions. Zevi was harshly critical of Ridolfi's vernacular "temptations," as well as the political components underlying his work (the Gramscian theory of national-popular culture in contrast to the avant-garde). On this, as on other occasion, Zevi negated his own most courageous and fertile attitudes. He had exalted Wright's example, where the creative impetus is taken from nature and the traditions of place, and yet in reality Zevi accepted the Wrightian point of view only in terms of the functionalist prejudice of "parthenogenesis," the idea of architecture reborn from within the fundamental framework of the historic avant-garde and definitively condemned to never look back, at risk of biblical transformation into a pillar of salt. The true biblical drama of Zevi lies in his absolute inability to reconcile his "truths" with the daily (and Platonic) application of history.

If, in the face of the above mentioned examples, Zevi showed tolerant reserve, even conceding the intrinsic quality of the work, he was completely closed to the Neo-Liberty movement which heralded the coming of age of a new generation, the architects born between 1925 and 1932. This generation was molded in the post-war period, and for them the battle for modern architecture and its "political difficulties" were merely vague childhood memories, acquired facts learned, with some suspicion, from elder brothers. This generation was "born pen in hand," with a great passion for rewriting history and for questioning and challenging the singular, accomodating point of view of the Modern Movement, which had the historians' seal of approval and was considered definitive and indisputable.

Neo-Liberty's clamorous explosion on the scene through the pages of *Casabella*, created something of an international furor. Issue number 215, put together by Rogers, published the work of a group of Turinese architects—Robert Gabetti, Aimaro Oreglia d'Isola and Giorgio Ranieri—for the first time. Among the works published was the celebrated Bottega de Erasmo, a building hidden, literally, in the shadow of Antonelli in a street of Turin. It had many characteristics which subtly linked it to traditional Piedmontese building types and yet also introduced explicitly assonant elements which made reference to the Amsterdam school, and to De Klerk in particular. Issue 215 contained a lucid and personal commentary by Gabetti and Isola, a subtle overview by Vittorio Gregotti and a paternalistic tirade by Rogers, which pointed up the many differences between the two generations. The Turinese spoke of their work not as a manifesto, or even a tendency, but rather as a return to architecture as a tool for understanding and for self-clarification, as a meditative and personal choice.

In fact, behind their understated and non-rhetorical manner, the Turinese could not hide the importance of their gesture, the extent to which it broke with the Modern Movement which had already assumed a defensive position. The Bottega di Erasmo, as well as other work in a similar vein, including that of Guido Canella, Vittorio Gregotti, Francesco Tentori and, in an autonomous position, Aldo Rossi, is the result of an uninhibited rummaging through the legacy of the pioneers of the Modern Movement, enriched by the activities of the "Italian school." This work goes way beyond the notions of historical dialogue which were acceptable to the modernist orthodoxy. From the moment in which the Modern Movement saw itself as a structure with a set direction, to be added on to by the superimposition of experiences, recycled versions of the initial experiences, the very pyramidal structure of the movement was called into question, tearing down its fragile theoretical skeleton, or verifying that it had already collapsed. There are separate and seemingly disconnected occurances during those years which, in hindsight, form a coherent picture. All over the world, and on the part of all generations, from the old masters to the most recent newcomers, there was a decisive change. Modern architecture, rootless in its constructivist utopia, came to be reconsigned to history as a phase in an unarrestable and unending dialectical process. The role of midwife fell, in addition to the great masters, to the Italians, who were not then suffering from "infantile regression," as Banham said, but were animated by their premonitions and imbued with a profoundly motivated doubt.

The Neo-Liberty movement unleashed a series of diverse reactions. The older masters first accelerated and intensified their historicizing, but then began to back off in progressive and suspicious fashion. Their retreat is not disconnected to the severe and absolute condemnation voiced by the critics. But the movement had a stimulating, and to a certain extent, liberating effect on others, demonstrated in Rogers' Velasca tower, Albini's Rinascente store, Gardella's church in Baranzate and Figini's and Pollini's house in via Circo.

In the first project for the Valesca tower, two boxey volumes are brusquely superimposed, and the circulation from one volume to another is left to the exterior structure. The final version incorporates inclined ramps and a plastic modelling of the large roof. This development demonstrates a logical jump which was able to occur under the influence of a new cultural climate, exemplified by the atmosphere surrounding *Casabella* after 1954, where there was an intense and productive reciprocity of experiences and influences between Rogers and his students.

In Albini's Renascente project there is also a change from the first to the second version which, while neither as radical nor significant as the change in Rogers' work, does demonstrate the prevalent effect of environmental considerations on structural and technological aspects. In the final version the external shell becomes a transcription of the classical order and an extremely elegant critique of the trilithic structure and the well-defined light and shade separation of the structural elements. Albini took his cue from the architecture of the city, extracting constant elements from it and reproposing them in a new manner, always careful to walk the fine line of technological justification. That justification finally assumes the role of an alibi, and the rippling vertical elements of the walls, similar to a blind colonnade which contains air conditioning vents, become a diplomatic gesture to neutralize the criticisms made in the name of orthodoxy.

Neo-Liberty, a phenomenon limited to the Padua region, (although significant echoes were felt in Naples, Florence and Palermo), never really assumed the characteristic of a tendency or movement, nor did it ever have a magazine at its disposition. In fact, after the violent attacks of Banham and of *L'Architecture d'Aujourd'hui, Casabella's* director issued an evasive and intimidated response and never gave the young architects the opportunity to make a personal rejoinder. In 1960 a group of young designers from Milan and Turin organized an exhibition of furniture which still adhered to the Neo-Liberty poetic, and the tone of the event was already defensive and justificatory, and it is significant that the work shown was not architecture but furniture. It became clear that they were giving up all thought of being a movement, and that they felt contrite at having allowed their "eager sentiments" (as Guido Canella wrote) to lead them down a "perverse" path.

"What seems to be missing"—wrote Vittorio Gregotti in the catalogue of the show, *New Designs for Italian Furniture,*—"in the architecture spectacle . . . is not so much the splendor of the light but the uncertainty of the shadow. A strongly optimistic smile (when it is not the professional smile of the salesman) seems painted on, from the false clarity which is the clarity of the object itself, to the closeminded certainty of the teaching. This smile hides an incapacity to recount what really is, or to acknowledge errors made or the doubts that plague our every day."

Who could ever be moved to tears by a chair? Making furniture has become as impossible as making a painting for a room; it is impossible, in any case, to do it with a clean conscience, without shame. Furnishing a house, one either chooses certain tools, (an armchair with a built-in egg beater, table, ice-maker, bed and television), or one attempts to represent a fact. And, should that representation finish in a farce, let us not forget that, after all, clowns have always performed a mediating role between mortals and the forces of destiny.

As for the purity of tubular chrome chairs, (which represents both an action and its definitive solution), one can substitute the desire for an image which is absurdly renewable, alluding directly to the user of the furniture, to an aging process which helps to annul the ahistorical nature of its birth, and which favors the possibility that the object will be overburdened with sentiments and meanings as if it had passed above time and events."

More or less during the same years that the Neo-Liberty polemics were articulated, other significant movements appeared in the chess match between the three forces in the Italian architectural world. The academics, nearing the age of retirement from university life, prepared to leave the scene and were preoccupied with questions of heredity. In Rome, the Chair of Composition, (which was the main discipline which concluded the basic course of study), was vacated by Foschini and remained empty while a successor was sought. Foschini, however, was not easy to replace. He had been nicknamed "The Cardinal" due to the protective and detached air which characterized his relationships with both colleagues and students, and he had always shown himself to be equitable and tolerant. In the profession, he had emphasized quality rather than quantity, without, however, ever moving too far from the "golden mean."

After long deliberations between Adalberto Libera and Saverio Muratori, the latter designated Foschini's successor. He was understood to be quite different from his predecessor, but "more our own," with respect to the sensibility of the academics. Libera, a member of "Group 8," had been one of the founders of "Italian Rationalism," sacrificing to the cause his own personal predilection for metaphysical architecture, imbued with magical presence. In the post-war period Libera had wed himself to an open experimentalism which, as a university docent, led him to embrace the idea of a technological utopia. Muratori had begun his career as an architect working together with Ludovico Quaroni and Francesco Fariello, and, after a series of extremely significant projects in the rationalist vocabulary, he participated with his partners in the great concession—EUR, assigning his group, along with Luigi Moretti, the central piazza. This was a scaleless project, in which the references to Scandinavian Neo-Classicism failed to compensate for a basic incapacity to achieve a dominant theme.

From the moment he assumed the chairmanship

in 1954, Muratori was outside the official architectural circles, and most of his projects remained on paper. In Pisa he built a church which remained unfinished, in which the local Romanesque style is transcribed with uncommon refinement in a basic, somewhat rarified space reminiscent of Plechnick's innovative work. Another building is under construction in Bologna which used a vocabulary evocative of the "Italian school." No one, however—not even the most prudent of his supporters—expected Muratori to inaugurate with his chairmanship a course of study which was a clear disavowal of the tradition of the Modern Movement. His teaching turned into not only a lucid theoretical denunciation of the contemporary crisis, but also a proposition for a restructuring from the bottom up of architectural theory and practice, based on an ambitious "scientific" theory of urban development as typological development.

The first courses of composition proposed by Muratori still hold the fascination of heresies. Using his closed and rigid system—the exact opposite of the tolerant and pluralistic didactic method of Foschini, his predecessor—one could refute all other methods, premises and consequences. One could not negate that Muratori's system expressed, with analytic profundity and archaic solemnity, the crisis of a culture which had fallen short of all its objectives.

The compositional exercises proposed by Muratori were elementary in nature and created an immediate negative reaction among the students. On the one hand they were asked to design a building with a central plan, using ancient masonry techniques so as to be freed from the equivocal structural "liberty" granted by modern techniques. On the other hand, they studied small scale residential units, "re-weavings" of the urban fabric which had been altered in modern times, using typological restoration methods, which would be used with great success in the historic center of Bologna some twenty years later. Muratori's greatest effort was to substitute for the old teaching method which had solicited originality and inventiveness, his objective, verifiable method, based on history. At first the students were more or less accepting, but they requested more open debate. Later there was a permanent rift between those who accepted and those who refuted a system which did not allow for discussion.

Under Muratori, the university was inflamed with controversy, and it was the academics themselves, still in control, who finally insisted that he give up some of his authority. They lined up, first behind Adalberto Libera and then behind Saul Greco, both of whom retreated from the courageous and arrogant hypotheses of Muratori. Muratori's message, pronounced within the closed walls of a university classroom, without the opportunity to grow or resonate through the pages of a magazine or through external debate which wasn't permeated by hyopcritical derision, was thwarted in its diffusion and development. His entire body of research came to be identified with and symbolized by one building, the headquarters of the Christian Democratic Party in EUR.

This work, the result of a long period of self-criticism, (more than thirteen solutions were studied and translated into models), reflects the anxiety of the designer who, wanting to exploit a professional opportunity, attempted to present a "portrait of power," shorn of every historical attribute. The result, both unresolved and a caricature, is a testimony to a completely cerebral approach to architecture. For this reason it seems to be the ghost of a project which never became true architecture, and the Christian Democratic party headquarters remains the unfortunate fruit of an anguished meditation on the crisis of civilization. It stands as a testimony to the "Muratorian heredity," free of ambitions to present itself as a conclusive and definitive solution to the crisis in architecture, and recognized as an interrupted message, therefore ambiguous and problematic, but engaging and questioning. This "inheritance", and in particular the emphatic focus on the culture of a specific site as well as certain elementary compositional motifs, warrants a comparison with the didactic and architectural work of an authentic master, Louis Kahn. Kahn, coming from a different and less sectarian context, was able to bring his instinctive ability as a builder to fruitful results which left their indelible mark on the architectural world of the 1960s.

Louis I. Kahn, Ayub National Hospital, Dacca, Bangladesh, 1963.

Louis I. Kahn, Indian Institute of Management, Ahmedabad, 1962, (photograph by J. Nicolais).

Pier Luigi Nervi, Vatican Hall, 1970.

Mario Ridolfi, Agip Motel project, Settebagni, Rome, 1968.

Gianfranco Caniggia, hospital extension, Isola-Liri, 1960.

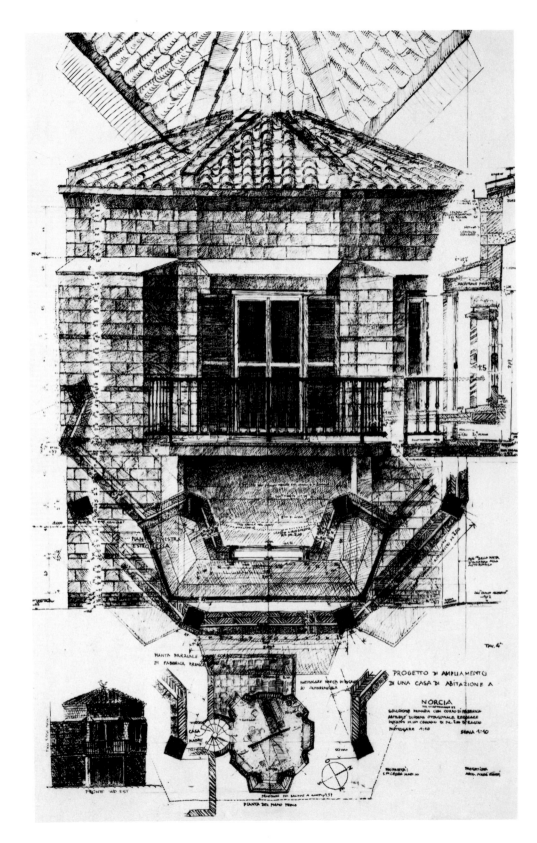

Mario Ridolfi, design for Otta-viani House addition, Norcia, Perugia, 1976–77.

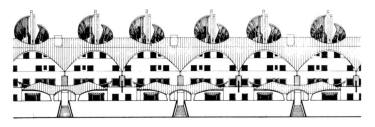
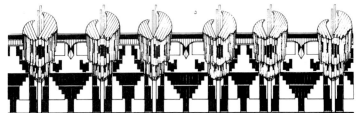

Ricardo Porro, Jean Robein, Jean-Francois Dechoux and Mohammed Rabbas, design, apartment house competition project Cergy-Puiseux.

Ricardo Porro, school of plastic arts, Havana, 1960.

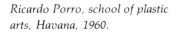

Ricardo Porro, school of plastic arts, Havana, 1960.

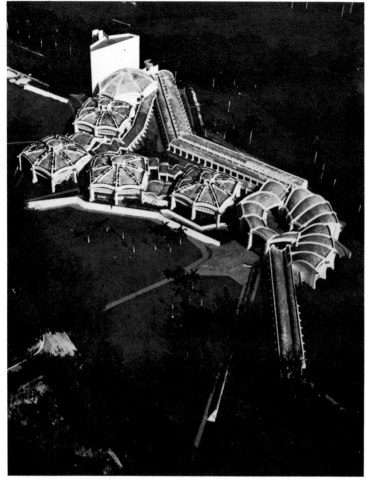

Ricardo Porro, dance school, Havana, 1962.

Roberto Gabetti and Aimaro Isola, model, project for a convent, Chieti, 1966.

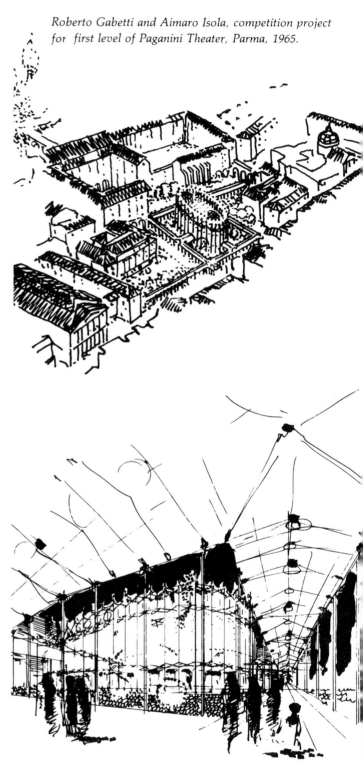

Roberto Gabetti and Aimaro Isola, sketch, competition project for first level of Paganini Theater, Parma, 1965.

Gottfried Böhm, town hall tower,
Bensberg, 1963.

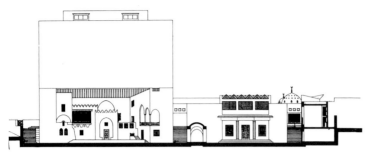

Hassan Fathy, project for a cultural institution, Luxor.

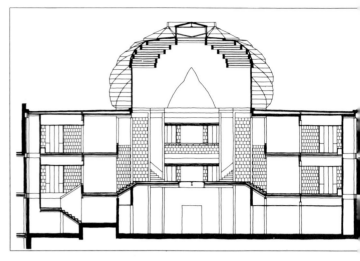

The Mandala Collaborative and Georges Candilis, cross section of a central space, project for Bu Ali Sina University, Hamadan.

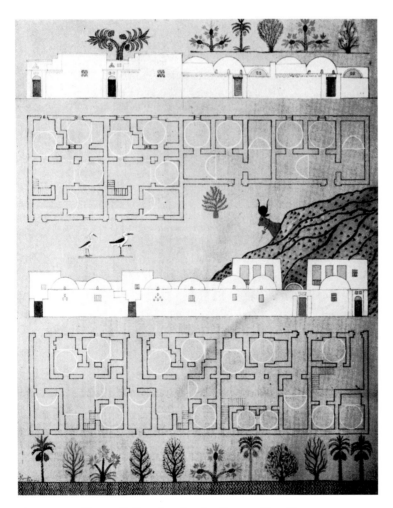

Hassan Fathy, drawing for Gourna New Town.

Roberto Gabetti, Aimaro Isola and Luciano Re, exterior view, villa, Pino Torinese, 1966–68.

Paolo Portoghesi, Baldi House, Rome, 1959.

Paolo Portoghesi, sketches for the commercial center, Vallo di Diano, 1980.

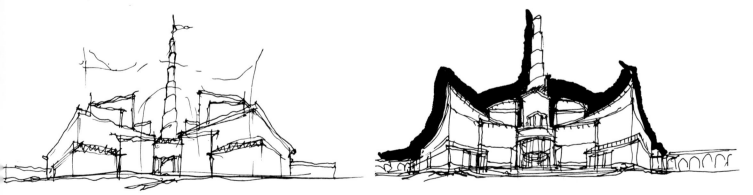

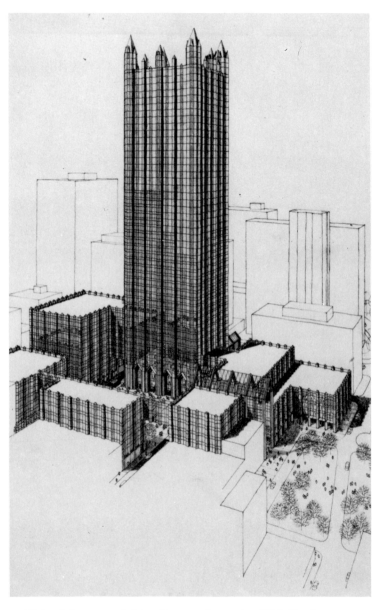

Philip Johnson and John Burgee, design for PPG Headquarters, Pittsburgh, Pennsylvania.

Philip Johnson and John Burgee, design for AT&T Headquarters, New York, N.Y.

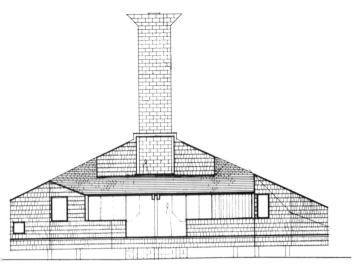

Robert Venturi, project for a beach house, 1959.

Robert Venturi and John Short, detail, North Pennsylvania Association of Visiting Nurses Headquarters, 1960.

Robert Venturi and John Rauch, Trubek and Wislocki House, Nantucket, Massachusetts, 1971–72.

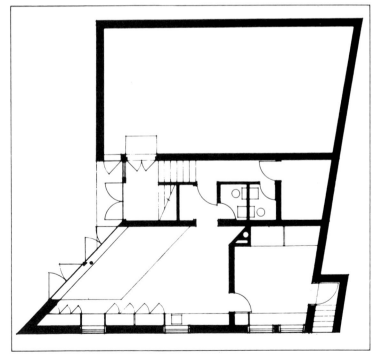

Robert Venturi and Short, plan, North Pennsylvania Association of Visiting Nurses Headquarters, 1960.

Robert Venturi and Short, house, Chestnut Hill, Pennsylvania, 1962–64.

Robert Venturi and John Rauch, facade for a house, Absecon, New Jersey, 1977.

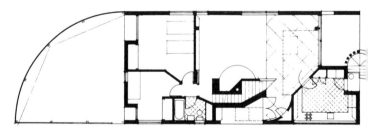

Robert Venturi and Short, plan, house, Chestnut Hill, Pennsylvania, 1962–64.

LEFT AND ABOVE LEFT:
Venturi & Rauch, two views of Franklin Court, Philadelphia, Pennsylvania, 1972.

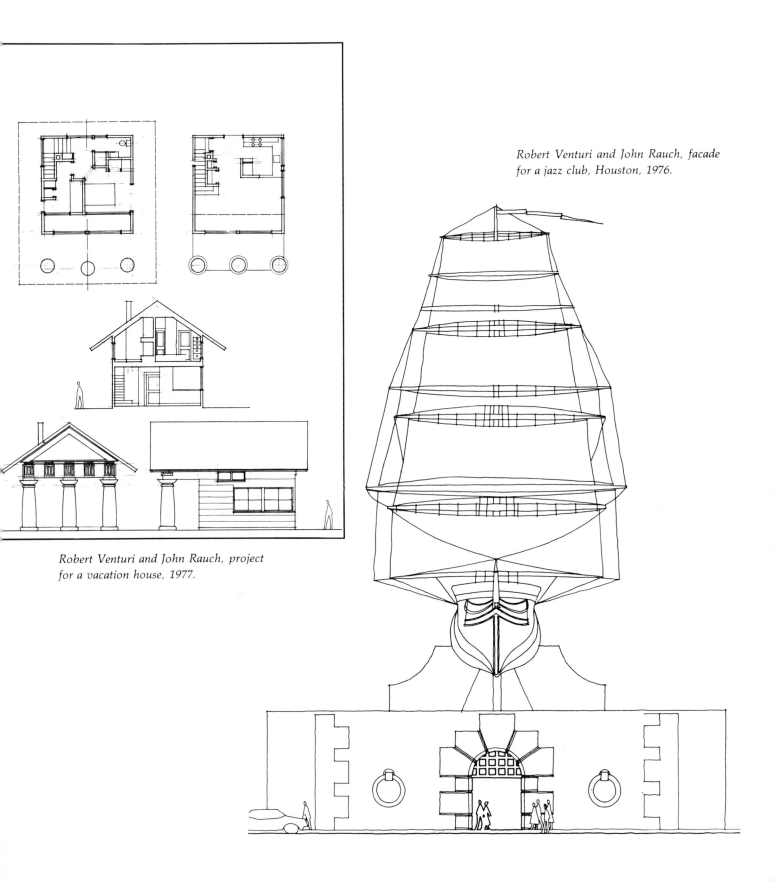

Robert Venturi and John Rauch, facade
for a jazz club, Houston, 1976.

Robert Venturi and John Rauch, project
for a vacation house, 1977.

Robert Venturi, interior view, Tucker House, New York, 1975.

Robert Venturi and Short, house, Chestnut Hill, Pennsylvania, 1962–64.

Robert Venturi, "Ionic" column, Johnson Gallery, Allen Memorial Art Museum, Oberlin, Ohio, 1973–76.

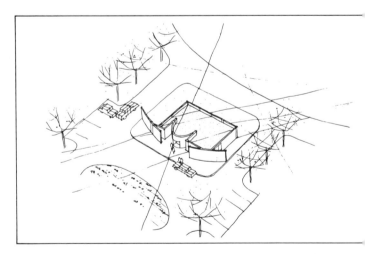

Robert Venturi and John Rauch, with R.J. Cripps, design for a building, Princeton Memorial Park, Highstone, New Jersey, 1966.

Charles Moore and Associates, exterior view, Keotz House, Westerly, Rhode Island, 1969.

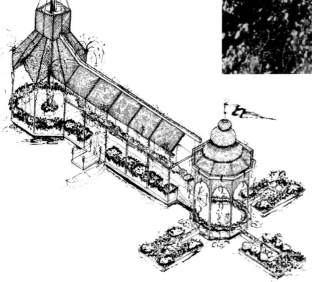

Charles Moore and Associates, two drawings for river bank project, Dayton, Ohio, 1976.

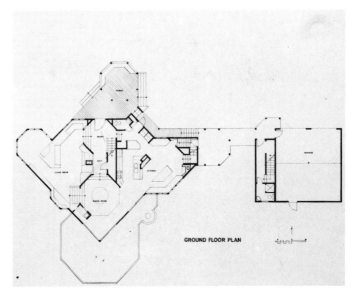

GROUND FLOOR PLAN

Charles Moore and Associates, plan, Keotz House, Westerly, Rhode Island, 1969.

Charles Moore, residential hotel project, St. Simons Island, Georgia.

Charles Moore and Associates, Faculty Club, University of California at Santa Barbara, 1968.

Charles Moore with Richard Chylinski, Burns House, Santa Monica, California, 1974.

Charles Moore with Urban Innovations Group, design for Piazza d'Italia, New Orleans, Louisiana, 1977–79.

Charles Moore and Associates, Gold Spring Harbor Guest House, Essex, Connecticut, 1979.

Charles Moore and Associates, Kresge College, University of California at Santa Cruz, 1974.

Charles Moore and Associates, Kresge College, University of California at Santa Cruz, 1974.

RIGHT:

Charles Moore and Associates, plan, Kresge College, University of California at Santa Cruz, 1974.

Charles Moore and Associates, river bank project, Dayton, Ohio, 1976.

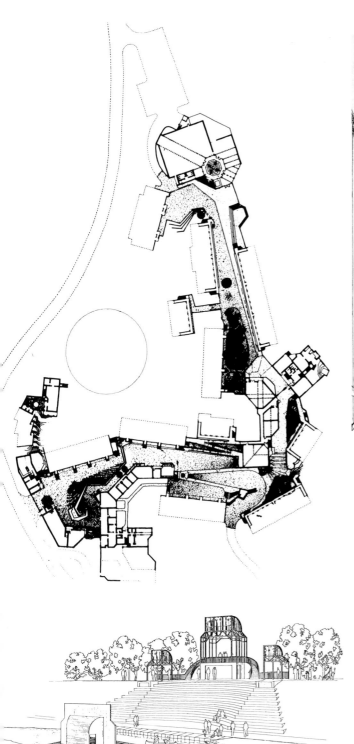

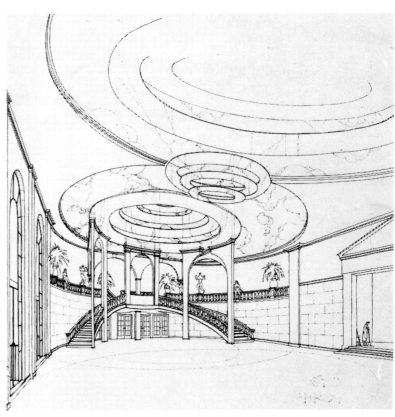

Charles Moore with Saputo and Rowe, drawing for interior of Italian-American Federation headquarters, New Orleans, 1979.

Charles Moore with Perez and Associates, project for Eola Hotel, Natuaez, Mississippi.

Charles Moore with Saputo and Rowe, project for the Italian–American Federation Headquarters, New Orleans, 1979.

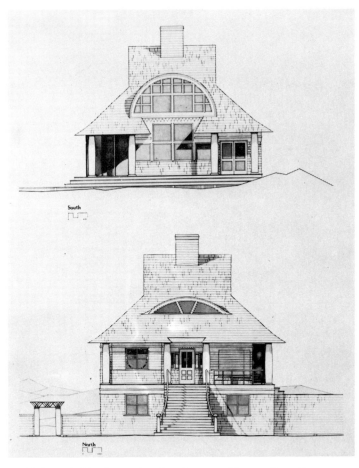

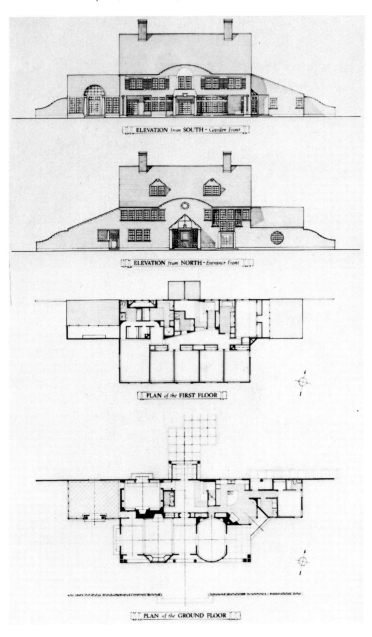

Robert A.M. Stern, elevations and plans, Brooks House, East Hampton, New York, 1979.

Robert A.M. Stern, facades, Lawson House, East Quogue, New York, 1979.

Robert A.M. Stern, facades, Martha Chilmark House, Martha's Vineyard, Massachusetts, 1979.

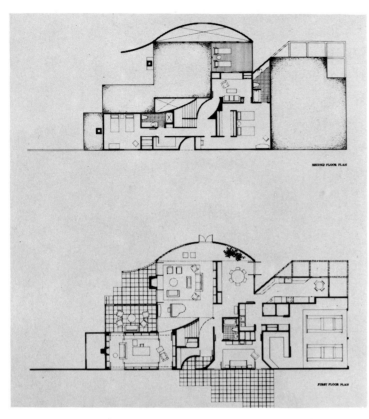

Robert A.M. Stern, plans, Lang House, Washington, 1973–74.

Robert A.M. Stern, axonometric view, Pool House, Greenwich, Connecticut, 1973–74.

Robert A.M. Stern, exterior details, Lang House, Washington, 1973–74.

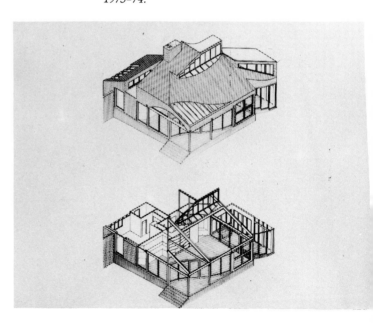

Robert A.M. Stern and John Hagmann, exterior view, West-chester House, Armonk, New York, 1974–76.

Robert A.M. Stern, interior detail, Jerome Greene Hall, Columbia University School of Law, New York, N.Y.

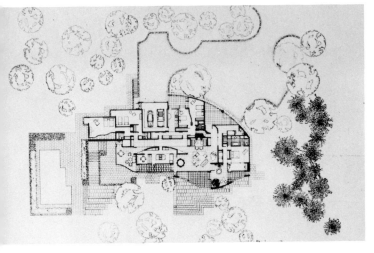

Robert A.M. Stern and John Hagmann, plan, Westchester House, Armonk, New York, 1974–76.

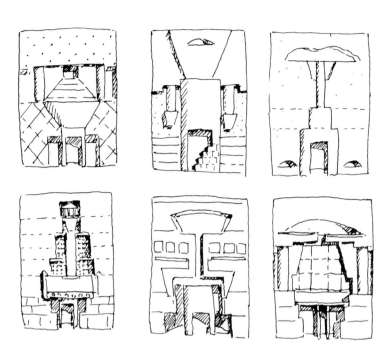

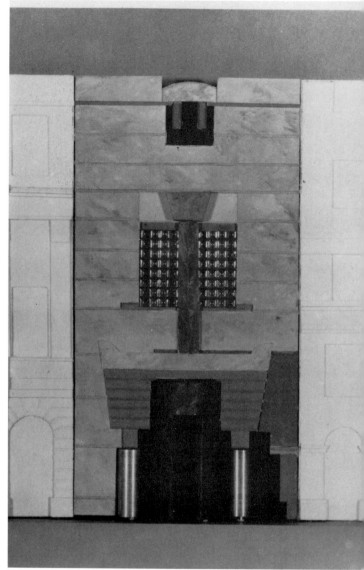

Michael Graves, studies for the facade of French & Company, New York, N.Y., 1978.

Michael Graves, project for French & Company, New York, N.Y., 1978.

Michael Graves, drawings for a vacation house, Aspen, Colorado.

Michael Graves, drawing for Kalko House, Green Brook, New York, 1978.

Michael Graves, project for the Fargo/Moorhead Cultural Center Bridge, Fargo, N. Dakota and Moorhead, Minn., 1978.

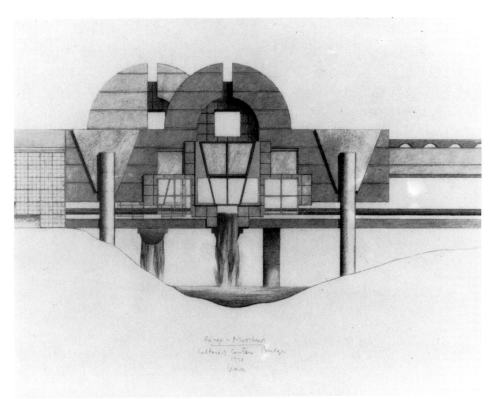

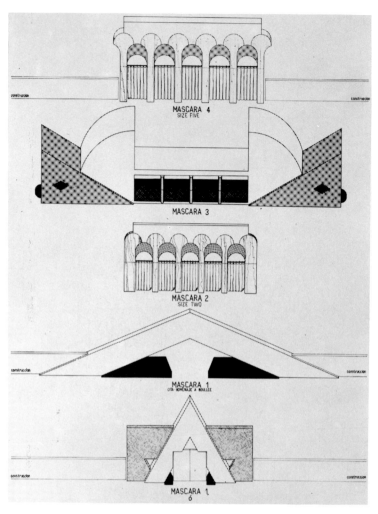

Rodolfo Machado, project for F/M House, 1972.

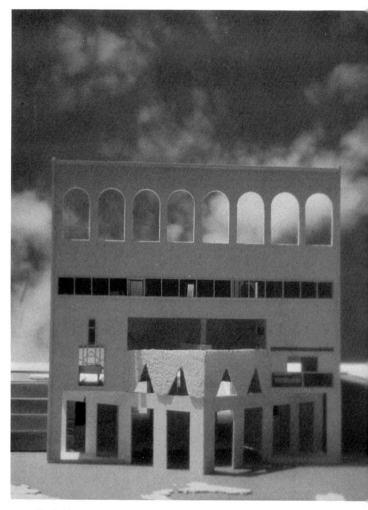

Rodolfo Machado and Jorge Silvetti, model, Fuente House, California, 1975.

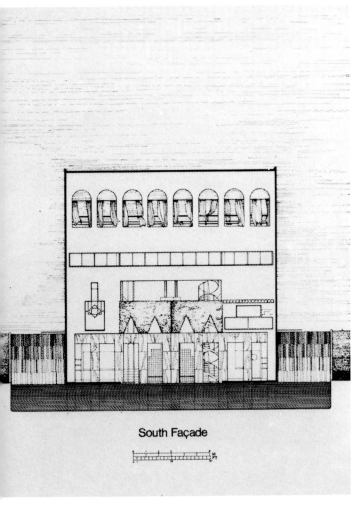

South Façade

Rodolfo Machado and Jorge Silvetti, south elevation,
Fuente House, California, 1975.

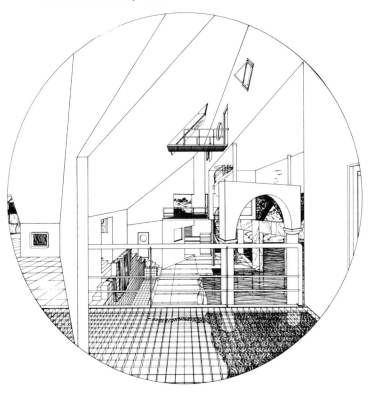

Rodolfo Machado and Jorge Silvetti, design of interior,
Fuente House, California, 1975.

Rodolfo Machado and Jorge Silvetti,
project for Frazier Terrace.

Allan Greenberg, exterior view, house, Guildford, 1978.

Diana Agrest and Mario Gandelsonas, project for a vacation house, Punte del Este, Uruguay, 1977.

Allan Greenberg, project for park pavilions, Manhattan.

William Turnbull, perspective view, project for a residential complex.

Taft Architects, project.

Andrew Batey and Mark Mack, project for an underground house, Napa Valley, California, 1979.

Andrew Batey and Mark Mack, project for a pavilion, Napa Valley, California, 1979.

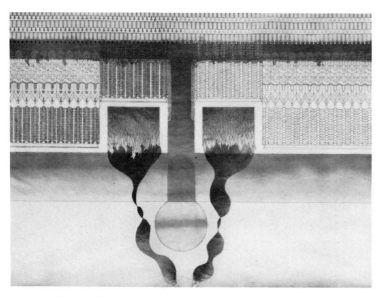

Stanley Tigerman, Pensacola Place, Project, 1973–76.

Stanley Tigerman, Baha'i Archives Center, 1976–79.

Stanley Tigerman, exterior view, Daisy House, Indiana 1975–78.

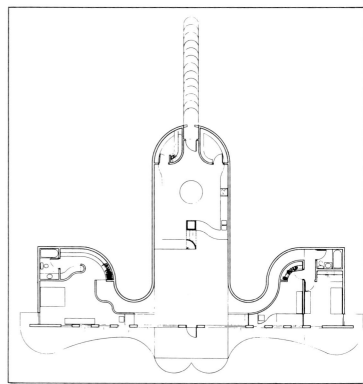

Stanley Tigerman, plan, Daisy House, Indiana, 1975–78.

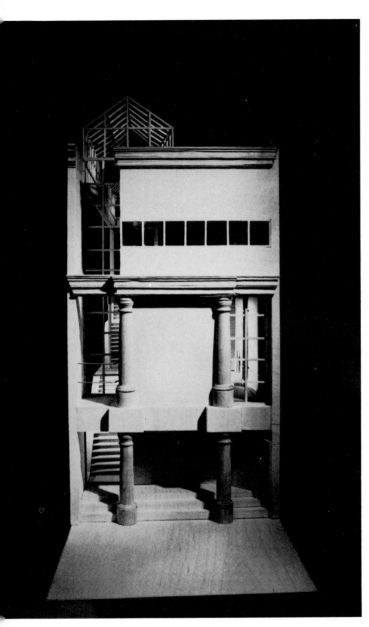

Beeby, Cohen and others, row houses for Kelly Gallery, Chicago, Illinois, 1978.

Stuart Cohen, townhouse project for Kelly Gallery, Chicago, Illinois, 1978.

Stanley Tigerman and Associates, model, Proeh Villa.

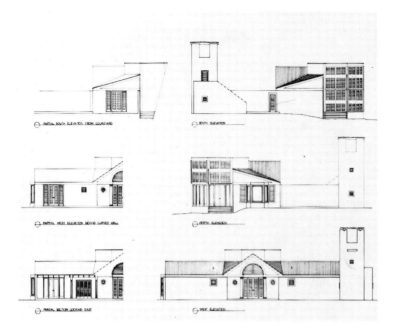

Hammond, Beeby and Babka, elevations and sections, Bush House, Harbour Island, Bahamas, 1979.

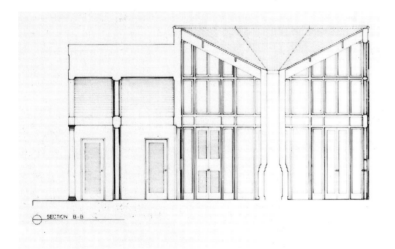

Kemp Mooney, Martha Brewer House, Atlanta, Georgia, 1979.

Thomas Gordon Smith, project for Paulownia House, Oakland, California, 1977.

Thomas Gordon Smith, James and Demetra Wilson House, Livermore, California, 1979.

Thomas Gordon Smith, project for Jefferson Street House, Berkeley, California, 1976.

THE AMERICAN SITUATION

It is necessary to differentiate three distinct periods in Louis Kahn's work. The first coincides with a long incubation, lasting until the mid 1950s. The second period, from 1955 until 1961, is explosive, extremely rich and contradictory, marked by his appearance on the American architectural scene with his projects for Philadelphia and the Richards laboratories. The third period is one of theoretical formulation and his most homogeneous and programmatic architectural work. During this last period he takes his place among the greatest American architects and assumes a mythic role of "poet of the institutions."

During the second period there were two developments in Kahn's work which were destined to have a profound effect on the architectural world. The first is his attitude toward the modern city, which he saw dramatically as a dialectical organism where chaos can be controlled only if one takes note of and studies the contradictions which emerge from it. His plan for Philadelphia calls for a reappropriation of the city by its inhabitants, based on their recognition of a barrier for vehicular traffic which becomes, in symbolic terms, a ring of towers like those that surrounded ancient walled cities. Kahn's second creative discovery in this period, which wasn't elaborated in his successive work, is his experimentation with a helicoidal spatiality of Piranesian complexity and ambiguity, realized in his tetrahedronal tower project, the "Tomorrow's City Hall" of 1957.

The last and most mature phase in Kahn's work is "fundamentalist." In his large-scale planning projects and in the volumetric complexes conceived as public institutions, he clearly distinguishes principal, "served" spaces from acillary, "serving" spaces, polarizing these elements and regrouping them with the distinctness and clarity of a crystal. The secret of this elementary and absolute quality, which evokes an Albertian sense of harmony, lies in the almost ritual character which Kahn attributes to the process of composing the parts into a whole. In any of his large volumetric projects of this period, one could trace the compositional history in "biblical" terms: "In the beginning was the square or cube . . . and the cube was divided into four parts according to its laws of orthogonal and diagonal symmetry . . . and the cylinders approached the cube, taking note of its corners . . .". Like an ancient military exercise on a battlefield, the Kahnian volumes give the impression of having attained their optimum strategic positions after a series of "operations," maneuvers which can be mentally reconstructed, almost as if they left a trace of their movements.

This methodology overturns the form-function relationship, assigning to the form the task of "evoking" the function as well as giving it the capacity to substantially modify that function. Kahn's writings are more poetic than theoretical, and they contain concepts, procedures and technical concepts which call for, first of all, a sense of "faith," a conviction which challenges the conditions of the present and reproposed a primary relationship, ingenuous and fundamental, between man and his creations, between man and nature. Architecture is that which nature cannot create; it is the sign of a mental order based on articulation, a thought made concrete. The progression from an inspiration to a human institution, to an actual space, is the journey of architecture, and it is accomplished by means of the individual creative act, deeply rooted, however, in the interpersonal values of the society.

In us
Inspiration to learn
Inspiration to question
Inspiration to live
Inspiration to express
These give to man his institutions.
The architect is he who creates spaces out of them.
The mind, the body, the arts bring these inspirations to light.
The mind, brain and psyche are the instrument which reveals the universe and eternity and, in the joy of the quest, poses the question, "why every thing?" . . .

Institutions are the houses of inspiration. Schools, libraries, laboratories, gymnasiums. The architect, before accepting the dictates of the requested space, considers the inspiration. He questions himself about its nature, what distinguishes one inspiration from another. When he has understood the difference, then he can be in touch with the corresponding form. The form inspires the project.

A work of art is the creation of a life. The architect chooses and composes to translate the institutions of man into environments and spatial relationships. It is art if it responds to the desire and beauty of the institution."

In addition to institutions, which interpret in spatial terms the various activities of man, the various moments of life, the conceptual act procedes from a series of archetypes which form the eternal present. Kahn is able to speak about these archetypes with simple eloquence, as if he were explaining to a child the reasons behind his profession, telling him fables which allow him to easily understand what would otherwise be difficult and confusing. It is sufficient to give a few examples to understand how much subsequent architectural debate owes to this disarming prophet, who was in large part repudiated by his followers. One needs only to read the pages dedicated to the column, the wall and the room, in which Hebraic inspiration, (as in so many other moments in more recent cultural history), is used as the irreplaceable tool for exploring the unknown.

Think about the great event of architecture, when the walls parted and the columns appeared.
It was such a happy event, and so intellectually marvelous, that nearly our entire architectural life derives from it.
The arch, the vault and the dome are signs of equally stimulating epochs, in which knowing how to do, one knew what to do, and knowing what to do, one knew how to do it.
Today these phenomena of form and space are as valid as they were yesterday, and they always will be, because they have shown themselves to correspond to needs and in the end have revealed their inherent beauty. . .
A column, when it is used, should always be considered a great event in the creation of space. Too often it appears only as a pilaster or a support. . .

"The wall that enclosed us for a long time until the man behind it, feeling a new freedom, wanted to look out. He hammered away to make an opening. The wall cried, "I have to protect you." And the man said, "I appreciate your faithfulness, but I feel time has brought change."
"The wall was sad, man realized something good. He visualized the opening as gracefully

arched, glorifying the wall. The wall was terribly pleased with its arch and carefully made jamb. The opening became part of the order of the wall."

Architecture creates the sensation of a world within a world, and it attributes this to the room. Try to think of the external world when you find yourself in a beautiful room with a fine person. All sensations from the outside world abandon you. I am reminded of a lovely poem by Rumi, the great Persian poet from the early thirteenth century. He tells the story of a priestess who was walking in a garden. It is springtime. The priestess stops at the threshhold of a house and remains dumbfounded. Her handmaiden approaches her exclaiming: "Look outside, look outside, priestess, at the miracle wrought by God." The priestess replies: "Look inside, and you will see God." It is a marvelous explanation of how one goes about creating a room. That which man makes, nature can not make, although man, to make it, adopts all the laws of nature. That which presides over creation and the desire to create, cannot exist in all of nature.

Kahn's concept of "room" implies a positive connotation of "closure," inverting the tendency to exalt every type of fracture and decomposition to the point where there is no distinction between internal and external. From here Kahn proceeds to a reacquisition of the notion of urban space and the street, expanding his verbal formulations beyond the scope of his projected or realized architecture.

The street is a room of agreement.
The street is dedicated by each house owner to the city in exchange of common services.
Deadend streets in cities today still retain this room character. Through streets, since the advent of the automobile, have entirely lost their room quality. I believe city planning can start with realization of this loss by directing the drive to reinstate the street where people live, shop and work as the room out of commonalty.

Kahn's compositions have a fundamentalist nature, whereby the guarantee of quality is tied to an elementariness, a clarity, an articulation of the relationship between the parts. The resultant complexity is always univocally reducible to a series of relationships instituted between primary visible forms and laws of virtual aggregation (axiality, transference, rotation, etc.). Kahn's teachings draw sustenance from its duplications and contradictory nature. This can be traced to his two sets of roots which are both antithetical and complementary: his Beaux-Arts education in Paris during the decisive, formative statute. Kahn's early teaching experience, which began at Yale in 1949, directly or indirectly involved many of the American protagonists of the "new architecture," from Robert Venturi (who studied at Princeton from 1947 to 1950 and then worked with Kahn until 1958), to Charles Moore (who received his doctorate and taught at Princeton from 1955 to 1960), to Tim Vreeland to Romaldo Giurgola (who worked at Kahn's side for many years).

From Princeton, from Yale and from Pennsylvania, where Kahn taught, his influence spread rapidly to nearly all the American universities on the east coast. His teaching was by no means limited to the traditional concept of the workshop. His students are all in agreement that his teachings are, in fact, a teaching methodology which transcends the coherent vision expressed by his work as an architect. One of the principles of this method, the concept of "deformation," give an idea of both the extent of the break with Kahn and the vastness of the influence of his teaching. Kahn, according to his students, distinguished between form and design, maintaining that form derives from both careful consideration of human activities which reveal themselves in a building, and from other needs of a functional order. Design, on the other hand, is a sort of imaginative reconsideration, tied to form, but with a strong degree independence. The primary act of architectural choice is a simple idea, a "strong idea" from which one arrives at the choice of a "form," drawing from the repertory of memory and from elementary geometry. This initial form is then rethought in terms of the human activities which will be carried out in relationship to it, and emerges out of this rethinking process, "deformed," adapted and made concrete at the same time. Only if this deformation is compatible with the laws of the forms and with human needs will the design process continue. If this compatibility does not occur, then one must choose another form and begin again.

This principle has, with respect to the methodology of the functionalist statute, the weight of a Copernican revolution, and it introduces a double dialectical movement into the linear progression supported by the Modern Movement. According to this principle, in fact, form is not born as a consequence of analysis and of a "list" of functions, but as an act of architectural will, as a choice internal to the discipline and its thought process. The problem of functions or, better, of "activities" comes up later, as a means for testing an intuitive act, the "choice of the form." At that point, one employs a specific mode of architectural thinking, the mental prefiguration of a problem by means of the evolutional representation of a form. In this way one no longer expects the function to generate the form, but rather the form, a choice from within the internal repertory of the discipline, to satisfy the function, and in creative fashion, to contribute something more, a redundancy, a tension. This is the gauge of the architectural character of the solution, indicating the extent to which the users will be offered an opportuniy for imaginative appropriation, whereby mind and body are one.

There is an oscillation from form to function and from function to form, which gradually tends to either ebb or stabilize at a point of equilibrium, whether static or dynamic. This dialectical vision restores to architecture a breadth of vision which the functionalist statute had denied, a freedom which is born out of intellectual tension and out of discipline, not out of the arbitrariness implicit in the mythology of novelty for its own sake. In this sense Kahn restores architecture, first to itself, and then to its history, rescuing it from the deadly embrace of technology and the risky identification of its figurative repertory with elementary geometry and abstract painting.

Louis Kahn streaked across the architectural sky like a meteor and, in the fifteen years which have seen the birth and the dimming of his trajectory, the world has changed profoundly, as has the role of architect, the conditions by which he works and his relationship with society. The poetic message of this fragile prophet, so full of faith and hope, can seem, in the wake of these changes, pathetically inadequate. But Kahn never meant his message to be closed and unilateral, a block of immovable truths. He sought a method, a profound tension which would lead to a reestablishment of the profession itself. And, indeed, his message has assumed diverse and unforeseen characteristics and results, through the work and the dialectical negation of his students. He has proven to be the only truly compelling force in the architectural debate of the last two decades.

Through the work of the heirs to Kahn, and in particular Venturi and Moore, one can slowly construct a tradition and a working method fraught with consequences which indicate, in different directions, a definitive way out of the orthodoxy of the Modern Movement.

Robert Venturi, the amiable and soft spoken proponent of the fertility of doubt, yet self-assured and incisive in his judgement, has become the ironic patriarch of a generation of architects who are radically changing the architectural panorama in the United States. Although he would not choose to be included as part of a movement and doesn't take pleasure in the company of followers, it would be simple to design for Venturi a leafy genealogical tree, with branches growing out from his teachings and his experience.

As early as 1959, in his project for a "house on the beach," designed under the influence of Kahn, he demonstrated a strongly creative conceptual approach and an already mature use of "recourse to memory." As Scully has revealed, the direct antecedent of the "house on the beach" is the Low House by McKim, Mead & White, one of the paradigmatic examples of the Shingle Style. Venturi, however, has introduced a series of "deformations" which change the meaning of the original. The unity and compactness of the original volumes are negated by an overall scheme which fragments the space, grouping together in an innovative fashion both rectangular and triangular prismatic structures. The resultant casual disposition of the subsidiary spaces is a marked contrast to the axial composition of the fireplace, emphasized by the gigantic chimney. Here, as in many other instances, Venturi seems to want his architecture to articulate differences in themes and eras. In this way all his projects, even those which seem to have feelings of nostalgia as their point of departure, become occasions to speak of the present, "affectionately" pointing out the difference between the bygone era and the model in question. It is a sort of dialogue with a father, for which one could easily write a plausible screen play, the design decisions are so clear and "logical." In the house on the beach the idea of the fireplace is the dominant theme to which the architect has tied the large sloped roof, which evokes memories of the Low House. But in order for this sacred space, heart of the house, to not appear distant from today's life, it is necessary to integrate it directly into the most banal functions of daily existence. For this reason the subsidiary spaces of the kitchen form an uninterrupted crown behind the chimney area. The diagonal cuts, on the other hand, with their uncompromising and problematic introduction of dead spaces, seem to negate any possibility of rhetorical interpretation.

The following decade sees the realization of Venturi's mature architectural vision. Charles Jencks has called his Headquarters Building of the North Penn Visiting Nurses Association (1960) "the first anti-monument of Post-Modernism." In this building there is a clear and explicit introduction of "complexity and contradiction" in the design of the architecture and its concrete results. Above all, there is the introduction of symbols drawn from the collective memory without the taboos of modern orthodoxy. The shallow cut-out arch which seems like a piece of cardboard asserts itself in front of the main entrance like an evocative sign, both emphasized and contradicted by the inclined beams behind. It is as though doubt itself, in the choice between one or the other of the possible solutions, comes to play an integral part in the built architecture. This is similar to what happens in the The Palace, where Giulio Romano places a triglyph of the architrave very low to the ground, in order to stress, by poking fun at them, the compositional rules. Duality and multiplicity play a role in the design process as well. It seems that Venturi, in still experimental fashion, wants to show that the only way to avoid the falseness of an obsolete ritual such as the modernist orthodoxy is to challenge its efficiency, its pleasantness, the ease with which it attains superficial and gratuitious "beauty" by means of coherence and a sense of organic unity. That organic unity, however, is so elementary in nature, it proves to be a simple tautology. Architecture will speak for itself, the Headquarters seem to say, and it is necessary, above all, to give up idiotic and inexpressive beauty, to discover the intelligence of the ugly, the provocative character and the communicative potential of the transgression. And so everything becomes different from what was foreseen and taken for granted. everything becomes "conquered" through modification. Even the celebrated ground level windows, which, with their molded cornices, seem to be fragments from a sixteenth century palace, take part in the game of unpredictability and contamination: they become a symbol of it.

In 1966 Venturi sincerely and clearly explained his tastes and his theories of architecture in *Complexity and Contradiction in Architecture*. The book was rapidly diffused throughout the English speaking world, and it was often compared to Le Corbusier's *Toward an Architecture* for the way the author embraces a new sensibility and points out to architects, as Le Corbusier did in his time, a whole reserve of experiences and meanings to discover and make use of. While the Swiss master identified this reserve in the spontaneous products of technology—hangers, transatlantic liners, port silos—Venturi locates his reserve at the center of modern American urban life—the culture of the masses, that totality of messages and signs which have modified the urban environment and which respond to certain primary necessities of a civilization based on information and communication.

Venturi's theoretical contribution is completely different from that of the masters of the Modern Movement and also from that of Louis Kahn. He does not present a systematic indication of what an architect ought to do, or poetic affirmations of universal principles to be followed. Rather, he offers an interpretive key to a series of architectural texts, drawn with great openmindedness from the entire repertory of architecture, from Greek civilization to the present, from autonomous works of architecture to more complex contexts where heterogeneous styles are tied together in a fabric, producing an aesthetic whole.

Along with these interpretive keys, Venturi offers the reader, with admirable candor, his personal judgments and predilections. He doesn't worry about showing his preference for the popular, and he relies on the reader's sympathy and the contagious nature of his ideas. He is convinced that his observations and judgments will find a spontaneous echo in the reader, since they are rooted in a wide spread collective sentiment, based on a reaction to a culture which, under the pretext of universality, has produced tragic results, having lost touch with the real world. The claiming of this new territory remains, to his way of seeing, the last hope for salvation of any cultural identity. One cannot really fault his views on the contagion of ideas and the presence of a new sense of reality. In the English speaking world, above all, Venturi's book has generated numerous "fashions," and his suggestions for re-reading pages from architectural history which have often been skipped over has led to clamorous revivals and veritable epidemics of interests.

Complexity and Contradiction, which Scully has appropriately termed an "uncomfortable work," begins with a "small manifesto" in favor of an equivocal architecture.

"I like"—the author states, dismissing any criticism of self-justification—"the fact that architecture is both complex and contradictory. It is not that I like incoherent and arbitrary architecture, the work of incompetent creators or the complications of taste rooted in the picturesque or in expressionism. On the contrary, I am speaking about a complex and contradictory architecture based on the wealth and ambiguity of modern life and the practice of art."

To his justification of a correspondence between complexity and the "spirit of the time," Venturi adds his belief in the aesthetic value of ambiguity, the salient characteristic of a work of art which sustains many different levels of meaning. William Empson's literary theory of "Seven Types of Ambiguity" furnishes many analogies and is used with great acumen by the author. The categories introduced, chapter by chapter, are interpretive tools and declarations of poetics, a means for analyzing the basic characteristics of taste, of the creative personality and, at the same time, a means for verifying which of these characteristics allow or reinforce spontaneous opinion.

As for the various levels of contradiction, Venturi differentiates the *both-and* phenomenon from that which he calls the element of double function. The first refers to the deliberate introduction of co-existing diverse characteristics in architecture. For example, the church of San Carlino by Borromini has an organization which is both central and longitudinal; instead of making a clear and unequivocal choice, Borromini has preferred a synthetic duplicity, which gives the work its extraordinary fascination.

We obey the tradition of "either-or" and we lack the agility of spirit—not to mention maturity—which would allow us access to the most subtle distinctions and hidden meanings, made possible by the tradition of "both-and." It is the "either-or" tradition which characterizes orthodox modern architecture: a parasole cannot in general be used for anything beyond its original intent, a support rarely serves as a covering [. . .] this way of manifesting the clarity and the good articulation of functions has nothing to do with an architecture of complexity and contradictions which seeks to integrate (both . . . and) rather than exclude ("either-or").

This "inclusive", as opposed to exclusive, poetic encourages refreshing contact with the culture of mannerism and the baroque. If inclusivity produces greater difficulties of interpretation, it is nonetheless valid in so far as it corresponds to the complexity of the subject matter. "Contemporaneous interpretations of numerous levels (of meaning) provoke in the observer attempts and hesitations which make his perceptions more alive."

If the objective of a complex architecture is to communicate along many levels of meaning, it then becomes essential for the architect to be familiar with the conventions of the general territory with which he will be dealing. "Today's architects, in their chimerical need to invent new techniques, have neglected this obligation: to be an expert in current conventions." The architect must use these conventions and make them live; his message will have the possibility of being understood to the extent that his work contains elements which are "known" to the users and which are capable of evoking series of analogous elements. The power of the classical architectural order lies precisely in its high degree of conventionality, in its presentation as a collection of rules which can be accepted or contradicted.

The principal task of the architect consists of the organization of a unique totality, based on conventional elements, judiciously introducing new elements when the old ones show themselves to be inappropriate . . . If he uses the conventions in an unconventional way, if he arranges common objects in an uncommon manner, he changes their context and can also use a consolidated type to obtain a new effect. Familiar objects placed in an unfamiliar context are perceived as new rather than old objects."

This investigation of the mechanisms of traditional communication in architecture has been used by Venturi to emphasize the impoverishment which provoked the rejection of orthodox Modernism in favor of a body of conventions which make up the traditional lexicon, a return to which can produce a repertory of forms which relate to a common visual experience, without distinction of epochs or styles. Pop Art demonstrates the importance of the banal object, and the possibility of its introduction into consciously artistic contexts.

As for the modern architects and planners who have reached beyond their grasp, seeking to invent and impose completely new environments and fail because they ask the impossible, Venturi proposes a different objective, less ambitious and more realistic. He proposes that they slightly revise the conventional elements of the urban landscape, profoundly changing the context and obtaining maximum results with minimum effort. It is a lucid and disenchanted reformist proposal compared to the revolutionary inclinations which have reduced the discipline to a desert of good but ignored intentions.

Complexity and Contradiction ends with a persuasive defense of the "difficult whole."

An architecture based on complexity and contradiction does not renounce unity. I attribute, in effect, particular importance to the creation of a whole because this whole is difficult to realize. And the goal which I seek is one of unity rather than simplicity in an art where truth resides in the totality. This is the difficult unity obtained by inclusion rather than the easy unity obtained by exclusion.

The book investigates the different modalities of this "difficult unity" which is seen as the result of a process: adapted contradiction, juxtaposed contradiction, contradiction between the external and internal form of a building, the inflection of the parts which influence each other in relationship to the whole. The discussion directly faces the problem of the environment and the city, since a building constitutes an autonomous unity which is, at the same time, always a fragment of a greater unity which must be taken into account in the design process. He takes a new theoretical approach which seems to derive its steps from a laboratory, and he makes headway in what has been jealously guarded territory in the discipline. He concludes with a modest but intense hope: that he has identified a more efficacious and realistic way for intervening in the real world, with the finality that is intrinsic to the human activity called architecture. "And it is perhaps in the every day landscape, vulgar and disregarded, that we will find the complex and contradictory order which is valid and vital for our architecture intended as an urban totality."

In his more recent work, Venturi vascillates between the establishment of a link with the regional American tradition and a discrete and extremely controlled use of modern vocabulary, always conditioned by the context in addition to the requirements of the clients, of whom some of his houses can be seen as veritable portraits. The Brant-Johnson house, in particular, built in 1976-77, is the culmination of his investigations and has the characteristics of a masterpiece. The tension between complexity and the ordinary, the banal, gives these architectural spaces a rare and convincing quality.

Beginning in the mid 1970s, Venturi's language becomes increasing obvious and wide-reaching in his use of recycled forms from the historic tradition. He achieves this not only through out of context references, but also through the integral adoption of traditional structural components, such as rustication and sequences of columns of pilasters. One could say, to paraphrase one of his own texts, that having completed the journey from Rome (where Venturi passed a crucial formative period during the 1940s) to Las Vegas, he is moving in the opposite direction, from Las Vegas toward Rome, and therefore toward the "re-use" of the conventions of classical language. In *Learning from Las Vegas*, the celebrated book which he wrote together with Denise Scott Brown and Steven Izenour, he chooses the model of the "decorated shed," to contrast with the "duck", (which typifies a building-sculpture in which the architectural system of the space, the structure and the layout are encompassed and distorted by an overall symbolic form). From this point on, he abandons all reserve with reference to the forbidden fruit of history, overcoming a line of demarcation which had been extremely clear for Kahn as well as the masters of the Modern Movement. Venturi, in fact, declines to rework historic forms, bringing them up-to-date by simplifying or transforming the original models. He limits himself to reproducing them, referring, however, not to their grand, "textbook" qualities, but to their image as it is debased through popular fantasy. This is his way of tapping the collective memory, resorting to caricature, to dialect and infantile interpretations, to the short-hand of comic strips—it is his way of turning toward Rome with the complicity of Las Vegas. One cannot ignore, of course, the influence on Venturi of Pop Art, but Venturi's vision is much broader, for it moves in two opposing directions— toward the banal, whereby situations from common, every day life are singled out, and toward the establishment of a system which sets off the Proustian mechanism of "involuntary memory."

The strength of Venturi's realism lies in the fact that he goes beyond the mere voicing of popular sentiments, always resorting to a double level of communication, cultured and popular, which confront each other and merge in irony, or, better yet, in "acuteness," or wit.

If we went to penetrate the conceptual laboratory of Venturi, beyond the sharp observations of Charles Jencks, we must refer to the "conceptism" of Gracián or to the Aristotelian "Telescope" of Tesauro. These two texts rigorously clarify the metaphorical processes and the problem of "popular" communication. For Gracián, wit is based on a tension and a discord between the extremes of a concept, that is, between the thought to be expressed and the objects which are posed as its equivalent. And Tesauro notes that "the art of the evangelical recitations lies in their relating in one breath both the easy and the difficult, which, in a populus composed of both intelligent beings and idiots, causes neither the intelligent ones to be fed up by over-explanations, nor the idiots to feel bored because they don't understand; this is the measure of true popular persuasion."

Take, for example, Venturi's project for a Jazz Club in Houston (1976). In the first version he proposed a classical facade with a central tympanum, a veritable "museum" which would set up a contrast between extremes—a recent and still living musical tradition and the museum as a temple to memory. This already indicated the mechanism of wit at work. In the final project a sailboat appears, hoisted up onto the roof, visible from great distances. The facade, meanwhile, has been simplified and looks like a marine warehouse, with a grand, rusticated entrance flanked by enormous rings, which allude to a metaphorical landing place. The progression from a purely conceptual metaphor to a metaphor-sign indicates his concern to project the building into its surroundings and to increase its communicative potential by means of unpredictability and a modification of the scale of objects (the boat, the rings). The historic image, (completed in the interior, with projections of old paintings), is then debased and nearly made into an indifferent consumer good, but is redeemed in the end by its very wit.

In the project for a house in Absecon, the use of an architectural order, redesigned in deliberately infantile and summary fashion, gives this "negligable" volume a character and an identity which stems from not the decoration itself, but the contrast between the decoration and the disposition of the windows, a mannerist and baroque technique, recaptured here with carping wit.

The other personality who stands out among the American exponents of the new architecture is Charles Moore. His work is deeply rooted in the concept of place, "place" intended not as a result of a simple arithmetical calculation—a specific space to which one adds the presence of man—but rather, "place" as the conclusion of a process of appropriation, to which architecture gives a ritualistic meaning.

Some of Moore's early houses have a "heart," as prescribed in Alberti's *De Re Aedificatoria.* These culminate in a kiosk, or baldacchino form, separable from the rest of the structure and held up by four wooden columns. It is a reversal of the *compluvium* of the classical house, a concrete articulation of one or more significant centers of the house which, in keeping with the character of modern life, have taken the place of the ancient contemplative center, the hearth.

Around this elementary archetype of baldacchino, the space which Moore constructs, with an exceptional variety of developments, winds around, opening up above and below with continuous pulsations. It is a space conditioned by the movements of the human body and often organized like groupings of stage sets. The architecture surrounds the body: it is seen as a backdrop for a complex activity; it sets the scene, not for heroic chance activities but for everyday life.

Proceeding from the discovery of a vital center for the inhabited space and from the notion of internal walls as screens designed by light, Moore adds what must be considered his characteristic compositional tool—the cut-out wall, matrix of both the internal and the external space. This becomes the fundamental element for recapturing, beyond any naturalistic evocation, a sense of "street" and "opening" which he accomplishes so skillfully in Kresge College. As in a street of a medieval city, the space is defined by a series of wings which angle off in different directions. Each one becomes, at a certain point, the background with respect to the foreground rhythm is developed, that of the cut-out windows, looking out on the background, and that of the cut-out screens of the loggias which unite the two planes. The result—also due to the harmony with the modification and miniaturization of the evoked model. His architecture is decidedly and intentionally figurative, and he searches for external references in the predilections of a client, his travels, his desires. A typical example of this dialogue between things and architectural institutions is the Piazza d'Italia in New Orleans, a pluralistic space designed for the local Italian community. The central element is a large fountain, a sort of dream-like disassembly of the Trevi Fountain, at the center of which there emerges the geographic profile of Italy. As a backdrop there is a large niche and a colonnade made up of five different orders, using forms and materials which accentuate its parodistic quality. Moore's diverting and transparent use of symbol culminates in the place of honor conceded to "Sicily" in the geographic profile. It coincides with the center of the piazza and can be used as a pulpit, acknowledging the fact that the majority of the Italian community in New Orleans is composed of Sicilians.

The choice of direct, almost scurrilous language, (redeemed by its dream-like quality), demonstrates the nearly limitless possibilities for recycling historic forms and arranging them in irreverent and transgressive montages. He has expanded the field, through an extraordinary fusion of narrative methods, finally making architecture open to certain aspects of the historic avant-garde, such as the ready-made and the use of historic references, which moralist purism had always excluded or censured.

In addition to this experimental work, Moore has made other courageous attempts to develop a personal language. In his of the vertical architectural elements, recurring in variable series, with the high tree trunks which define the landscape—is one of the most valid and rich examples of American architecture to come out of the rejection of the orthodoxy of the Modern Movement.

Moore's theoretical contribution, likewise, centers on the theme of the house, the body, memory. His empirical tone and his faith in his profession sets his writings apart from those of all the other architects of his generation. His main concern is to restore the power of the word to architecture, long silenced by obedience to moralistic or technological factors. To accomplish this he seems willing to take any risk, to expose himself to any influence.

He expouses his principles of place in his book, *The Place of Houses*, written in 1974 with Gerald Allen and Donlyn Lyndon. Along with *the order of rooms* and *the order of machines*, which develop Kahnian premises, Moore introduces *the order of dreams*, to which he dedicates a chapter filled with humor and wisdom.

The arrangement of rooms can offer a context for daily activities and, putting the fixtures in order, one can dignify specific activities. But to construct a good house it is also necessary to pay attention to another aspect. Dreams, which accompany all human actions, must be nurtured by the places in which people live.

For Moore, the most simple and natural way to express the "order of dreams" is to utilize "memorable" things from other times and other places, a recourse to memory, therefore, but Headquarters for the Italian-American Federation in New Orleans and the Eola Hotel in Natuaez, the compact volumes are qualified to the extent that there is a relentless ambiguity in the reading of the parts and the whole. His planning projects are no less promising. His plan for the riverfront in Dayton expresses his irrepressible theatrical streak, as he animates the festive spaces in fantastic, provocative fashion. Even here Moore remains faithful to his proclaimed principles:

My principles derive from a conviction that the act of habitation is a primary experience of man, on a par with food and sex, and this need can be satisfied only by the joint efforts of user and designer. That is to say, the role of the architect consists, appropriately, in the establishment of a series of familiar environments which give the inhabitant the possibility of connecting with everything around him, with the help of a series of surprises which bring him to a greater understanding of the place where he finds himself.

I believe that the architects of this century are too rooted in the fascination of the reassuring effect of that which is familiar. It follows that, if the act of habitation must be facilitated and not inhibited, it is necessary that houses can and must speak to their inhabitants. It is necessary, therefore, that we have free use of language to transmit messages of any type, diverting or engaging, serious and ironical, frivolous or important. Since most architects don't agree with this principle, I am forced (perhaps excessively) to investigate the "strange" and the "unusual" (within the reassuring limits of that which is familiar).

Another basic principle for me is that the human body (and not only the eyes) constitutes the most important and central element which helps us to locate ourselves in a space; the notions of over/under, right/left, in front/behind/center are more fundamental to human existence that any abstraction such as the cartesian coordinates. As for images, every architect has his preferences which, even if he can't justify them with principles, they can still be strong enough to give form to his work. My preferences include the geode, the Russian Easter egg, the surprise of a crystal inside a rough shell, and the "false" facade, which I usually cut out in such a manner that, through this external screen, one can glimpse fragments of the body that lies behind.

At the beginning of the 1970s, an apparent alternative to the directions taken by Venturi and Moore seemed to be offered in the work of the New York Five. At a meeting organized by the Museum of Modern Art in 1969, Kenneth Frampton presented the work of Peter Eisenman, Michael Graves, John Hejduk, Charles Gwathmey and Richard Meier as a homogeneous phenomenon. The group then received official approval in 1972 with the publication of a book by Arthur Drexler in which he singled out the common denominator of their work in their negation of both brutalism and emphasis on contents, and in their return to the "semantic specificity of architecture."

The work of the New York Five was rapidly disseminated, acquiring renown and in a certain way echoed by the Neo-Rationalist movement in Europe. But the issue which held the group together—the recycling of the rationalist language of Le Corbusier and Terragni—while resulting in an obvious flowering of work, was destined to rapid obsolescence, and its possibilities were exhausted, in adapted fashion, in the work undertaken by the early disciples of Kahn. One could say, in fact, that the use of language proposed by the Five is both neutral and asemantic. It proposes not a revival, but a re-reading, *a posteriori*, of the achievements of the Modern Movement. But it is also true that once a decision has been made to look back at rationalism as a thing of the past, one is no longer obliged to adhere to its rigid, Manichean limitations, and, using Kahn as an example, one can choose to restore modern architecture to the embrace of history. The work of the Five lacks the crucial factor of "contamination," which exploits the potential difference between the ancient and the modern, thereby adjusting to the new socio-cultural reality. It is no accident that their manner of being up-to-date, still fraught with inhibitions and fears, has been sponsored with cruel enthusiasm by the priests of negative thought. The long agony of the Modern Movement has thus taken the form of a delirium, in which the veiled and stiffened dreams of a happy childhood appear, as in super-realist painting.

This apparently progressive evolution reveals itself to be, in the long run, sterile and opportunistic; it guarantees the success of a fashion, but omits the possibility of fertile development. Semantics have been substituted by rhetoric, and a poverty of references by absolute silence. Forms which had symbolized a hope to change the world are used to demonstrate the fact that it cannot change, a device meant to implement a return to quality and to express diversity, compared to prevalent dispersive pluralism. But this also became proof of persistent doubts and inhibitions, as can be seen in the diaspora of the Five with respect to the dogmas which initially held them together. While Eisenman obstinately continues his experiments in a void, moving like a condemned man in his cell among the shadows of Le Corbusier, Rietveld and Terragni, the others have either been off target or have chosen the path of professional popularization, or, like Graves and Hejduk, have judiciously and independently moved toward a riskier but less sterile approach.

Graves, in particular, abandoning the new dogmatism, abandoned a veiled and ambiguous identity to reveal one of the most fertile and problematic personalities on the American scene today. Through his work he merges a reexamination of classical archetypes with a decomposition of form and, in his anxiety to establish some communication with the user, he heightens both the frontality and the representation of depth of the space. His drawings, which attempt to imbue the basic volumetric play with the ingenuous clarity of a child's construction, are among the most successful examples of a recodification of architectural language anchored in the collective memory.

Robert Stern is an equally decisive figure who has abandoned American neo-rationalism, following his predilection for a New Shingle Style. He merges the visual eloquence of the Five with an uninhibited and radical tapping of both historic references and American roots. Stern has articulated his principles with pragmatic clarity, elucidating his methodology, which is marked by its absence of ideological components.

1. The application of decoration is not a crime.
2. Buildings inspired by other buildings in the history of architecture are more significant than those which have no inspiration (this was once called "eclecticism").
3. Buildings which relate to surrounding buildings have more power than those which don't relate to them (what was once called "common courtesy" could also be called "contextual integration").
4. Buildings which are tied to ideas of the specific facts which have produced them are more significant than those which don't have such ties. It is legitimate, not only to investigate specific images to communicate ideas about buildings, but it is also possible and logical to simultaneously project two distinct buildings, with one result being different from the other.
5. Architecture is "story telling" or a communicative

art. Our facades are not transparent veils, nor are they the affirmation of profound structural secrets. They function as mediators between the building in its "real" construction and those illusions and perceptions which are necessary to place buildings in closer relationship with their places of construction, with convictions and dreams of the architects who have made them, with the clients who have paid for them, and with the civilization which has allowed them to be built.

We believe that architectural design is, in part, a process of cultural assimilation, but also an attempt to suggest that today's problems do not consist in the discussion of functional and technological paradigms established for the great majority of paradigms which continue to pester us after the end of the modern movement. This sort of discussion cannot come from the talent of an individual architect alone: history, the state of the architectural art at a given moment, the aspirations of clients, all these must assume a role in the architectural design process. It is necessary to repeat the affirmation that single buildings—no matter how distant from other pieces of architecture—are part of a cultural and physical context and we, as architects, are compelled to recognize these connections in our theories and in the combination of forms which we establish in that which we too casually call 'design.'

Our attitude toward form, which is based on a love for history and an awareness of it, does not imply accurate reproduction. It is eclectic and is used as a technique of collage and juxtaposition, to give new meaning to known forms and thereby goes off in new directions. Our faith is in the power of memory (history), combined with richness and meaning. If architecture is to succeed in its attempt to creatively participate in the present, it is necessary that it overcome the iconoclasm of the last fifty years of the modern movement or the limited formalism of so many recent works, and that it reclaim a cultural base and the most complete possible reading of the past.

With these premises, which do away with intellectual snobbery, Stern and his collaborators have realized various houses which are extraordinarily fascinating, in which the skillful theatrical approach is united with a refreshing spatial and luminous inventiveness and a rigorous grammatical control.

At the onset of the 1980s, the contemporary American panorama is extremely open and promising, and the orientation of the younger generation is increasingly distant from the tired professional reelaborations of the International Style and from the myths of technology for its own sake. A notable group of creative personalities has opened up the universities and brought in a breath of fresh air. They shared in common a recognition of the necessity to build on the ashes of the Modern Movement, to establish a culture capable of responding to the new needs of a profoundly changed society.

To conclude our essay, which doesn't even pretend to hypothesize about developments which are still in their early stages, we must mention the names of Agrest-Gandelsonas, the Taft group, Stanley Tigerman (who, from an autonomous position, has enriched the landscape in an ironic vein with his strongly figurative work), and the Machado-Silvetti group, authors of the suggestive Fuente House, one of the most creative applications of the use of metaphor. Finally, Thomas Gordon Smith, still in his early thirties, is perhaps the most audacious and decisive in his creative use of memory. His images, which revive the doubts and witicisms of Giulio Romano, together with a fluid reworking of baroque and expressionist spatial prototypes, are among the most eloquent examples in a wide open field which has seen the end of the last inhibitions on which the prestige of an authoritarian orthodoxy had rested.

THE EUROPEAN HORIZON

If in the United States, beginning with Kahnian reform and Johnson's declaration of principles, it is possible to establish a continuous line of development from the end of the 1950s until today, the European panorama, on the other hand, presents us with a series of vacillating movements, hesitations and renunciations. These are symptoms of a dispersive and contradictory debate which has only in recent years begun to go someplace.

At the beginning of the 1960s a fair number of Italian architects were working their way out of the orthodoxy of the Modern Movement. The leaders of the middle generation—from Ridolfi to Michelucci, Albini and Gardella—were particularly engaged in unbiased confrontation with history. The group of younger architects who gave birth to the Neo-Liberty movement were working along similar lines—Gabetti, Isola and Raineri in Turin; Gregotti, Canella, Rossi and Aulenti in Milan.

The convergence of these tendencies, however, did not constitute a decisive and theoretically mature front. The rallying cry of the defenders of modernist orthodoxy brought about, within the span of a few years, an unexpected erosion of positions. Meanwhile, new myths were hurriedly coined to bury the still nascent reformist attempts, which were, on the other hand, compromised by populist elements. The new myths were those of emerging technology, the total industrialization of the building industry and "urbanism," that is, urban planning by means of *zoning*—the definition for that organic area between architecture and politics, between design and society. The great

myth that the world might be redeemed through architecture was thereby brought up to date, substituting planning for architecture and therefore degrading architecture as some frivolous and changeable appendage to the planning process.

The so-called European "economic miracle," meanwhile, brought along a gust of utopian air and an acritical faith in development as progress. Many architects, old and young, were inclined to remove themselves from their true profession and from an understanding of social realities, to venture along the easy paths of social engineering, the more or less gratuitous invention of a new world, inhabited by men who had been custom designed to live there.

The reactions of the "masters" were, if varied, similar in result. Michelucci sought refuge in a primordial reality, almost as if history could only be dealt with from an enormous distance. Albini, abandoning his daring recycling of historic elements, seen in his San Lorenzo museum and in the Rinascente department store, became ever more entrenched in a discrete and cautious endeavor: the redesigning of a technological vocabulary in pleasingly elegant fashion. Gardella, too, seemed to slow down after his principal achievements—namely his Venetian apartment house in Zattere and the Olivetti dining room—deliberately hiding behind private and minor statements, the most significant being his work in Arenzano.

Scarpa and Ridolfi took a different route. The former, tireless in his efforts to clarify a syntactical method for the piece by piece transcription of themes and concerns of the Venetian tradition, has never given up his attempts to probe and distill the mnemonic roots of architecture, breaking them down, altering and pushing them to the point of exasperation. He uses the art of memory to reduce a text to an allusive shorthand, moving from Venice toward a symbolic destination in the Far East, seen through the filter of Zen thought.

In the mid 1960s, Ridolfi, like Scarpa, cut himself off from the current architectural debate. His detachment, however, has never stemmed from an aristocratic pursuit of ideals of quality, but from an obstinate eternal return to his favorite themes—the house and a sense of craftmanship which, verifying architectural form, restores it to its cultural/material roots. His work exemplifies a convergence of manual and mental labor. Forgotten by everyone, save a few friends who continue to see him as the stabile center of a culture in flux and those who have visited him in his provincial exile in Marmore, Ridolfi has built houses which have the formal perfection of a sonnet and the internal animation of the ballet. In all his work there is the reappearance of vocabularies dug up from the collective memory and reproposed, as though reborn, from the internal logic of his design process.

Gabetti and Isola, the leading spirits behind the Neo-Liberty movement in Padua, have continued their work at a very high level. Gradually however, they have removed themselves from polemic issues, giving the impression that rather than cross into new territory, they would prefer to explore the limits of orthodox modernism.

Vittorio Gregotti has more clearly and irrevocably turned his back on the Neo-Liberty movement. Beginning in the late 1960s he, and other Europeans of his generation and pursuasion such as Ungers, Alvaro Siza and Oriol Bohigas, drew attention to themselves for their efforts to reestablish a rationalist approach, in contrast to the dispersed pluralism of the modern movement. Seeking to demystify the design process, Gregotti has applied himself to the development of a body of work influenced by a technological vocabulary, choosing to never cross the threshold beyond elementary geometry and a certain predilection for the "look" of masonry construction. As in the case of Eisenman and Meier, Gregotti's break with orthodoxy lies in his employment of examples of classical rationalism from the 1920s and '30s as historical material, as a dead language used for syntactical and rhetorical exercises, chosen specifically for its "emptiness" and lack of symbolic contamination of mnemonic depth, and therefore particularly appropriate for a program of "austerity." This approach limits neo-rationalism to an inhibited recapitulation of the recent past and lacks the provocative dialectics of the more authentic examples of Post-Modernism.

Aldo Rossi, the most fascinating figure on the European architectural horizon, appears at the limits of Neo-Rationalism. He has realized few buildings, none of which has the quality of a masterpiece, but his drawings and projects are eloquent testimony to the apprehensions and doubts, but also certain rediscovered truths, for an entire generation of architects. At the end of the 1950s, Rossi was, in tangential fashion, a member of a group of Rogers' students who participated in the Neo-Liberty movement. He was, however, the first to clearly see the limits of that movement, the lack of opportunities for development. His intellectual passion for the rigors of Loosian thought made him suspicious of the personal, psychological approach of his peers. He was also clearly distinguished from those who advocated a return to functionalist orthodoxy by his vision of architecture's historical division of culture into two time frames—before and after the advent of industrial production and the Modern Movement. In a letter, reprinted by Francesco Tentori in the catalogue for an exhibition in Aquila in 1963, he already makes clear, along with the principles behind his poetics, the differences which separate him from the true Neo-Rationalists:

In my projects or writings I try to establish a rigid world with few objects; a world with given facts already understood . . . If I could say simply what interests me about architecture, I would say that I am interested in the problem of knowledge. Why in architecture? Probably because architecture is my profession, and for no other reason . . . nor do I believe that one can have a calling to architecture, or to any other field; it is simply a problem of different skills to be learned as best as one can.

. . . this type of position negates, and ignores, the entire issue of "redeeming" values which the Modern Movement has been inclined to attribute to architecture or to art—both in terms of attitude and of formal result. For this reason, and not because of polemics, but rather because I have another view of the problem, I have never distinguished between modern architecture and something else; that is, I simply proceed to choose among certain types of models. The only difficulty, then, lies in the description. We all have an idea of an ideal model and we believe that we can describe it in ideal or typical fashion. Instead, in the moment when we describe it, we reveal our incapacity to do so, and the greatest results are achieved when we get closer to the idea itself. In any case, the translation of this idea offers a group of representations from which we cannot remove ourselves. The forms which we lend out, or which are representations themselves, endure. This permanence of form is, perhaps, all that we can grasp or express of reality.

This is the period when Rossi, having left "Casabella," withdrew into his studio to develop his theoretical and practical vocabulary which brought him to the forefront of those who were outside the mainstream of architecture. "A rigid world with few objects" is the formulation of a reductive program which will be meticulously put into effect over the next fifteen years of work. His is a world of elementary forms which, while drawn from geometry, pass through the filter of history, in an attempt at identification which can occur only by appealing to consciousness, to mental images, to the archetypes which make up the collective memory. The column has its archetype in the cylinder; the tympanum and the sloping roof are likewise distilled into an equally elementary form, a prism generated from an equilateral triangle. The window is found in the square, a form in which only two dimensions prevail, the most simple forms which has an autonomous balance. The cupola, by this process of geometrical identification, becomes a hemisphere or a pyramid. The wall, made up of filleted sections, can enclose parallelepipeds or prisms based on polygons. Rossi's compositional method is based on the atonal and unexpected assemblage of these archetypes which can be clearly rearranged as forms which have flowered from memory and which can be used to interpret new architectural possibilities.

As for the absolute simplicity of the elements employed, one could assume that Rossi arrives at his forms by successive simplification. But this is in strong contrast to the unpredictable and complex manner in which the forms are either juxtaposed or interpenetrate, placing them at considerable distance from classical compositions. These relationships which Rossi seeks express a difficult, "hard-earned" condition, which comes close to, but always ultimately avoids, banality. In metaphysical and surreal painting, the object, without specific quality, is sublimated and repressed by the magic of light and decontextualization. In analagous fashion, in Rossi's architecture, objects become expressive and surprising by the provocative stillness and richness of associations.

Rossi's writings which accompany his projects are very explicit and offer valuable interpretive keys to the character of his associations. For example, referring to the exhibition in the park for the 1964 Triennial, Rossi speaks of a "reference to archaeological sections, with their ordered freedom, or that disorder which lies in an order which can no longer be completely traced in the excavations." Speaking of the Scandicci town hall, he refers to industrial architecture and to "certain constants" in Tuscan architecture; while, in the case of the house in Ticino, he states that "the associations for this project are as numerous as the forest and lake constructions and finally relate back to pile and industrial structures (bridges, quarries, dams, etc.) which are characteristic of the landscape of the Alps and their foothills." In his project for the business district of Florence, his recollection of historic form is more explicit (the baptistry, the towers), but is always tied more to types than to particular aspects of a given monument.

The culmination of this referential poetics is Rossi's "Teatro del Mondo," in which Eastern memories coexist with references to Carpaccio, as well as allusions to America. Rossi has written:

The barges that descend from Ticino are transformed in the fog of Lombardy into carnival boats, the water structures bear traces of the Gothic cities to the North. The Limmat, the river which crosses Zurich, was filled with houses or towers which were warehouses, repositories, but also mysterious places, iniquitous, suspended between water and land.

Oriental cities were and are surrounded by this world of barges. Venice, synthesis of Gothic and foggy landscapes, with pieces or transpositions from the Orient, establishes itself as the capital of water cities, and therefore, of the possible landscapes, (and not only physical or topographical), between the two worlds. Even the Rialto bridge is a landscape, a market, a theater.

In designing a building, these analogies of place have decisive importance for me; if well interpreted, they are already the design.

The "analogies of place" *are already* the design: this is the most reliable clue for understanding Rossi's method, "the art of memory," and for heeding the natural inclination of places which continuously express their true roots.

Jung has written (according to Savi in his monograph):

Logical thought is thought expressed in works, which are outwardly directed like a conversation. Analogical or imaginative thought is sensitive, figurative and mute, not a conversation but a material rumination through the past, a turning inward. Logical thought is thinking with words. Analogical thought is archaic, unconscious and not expressed, and practically inexpressible in words.

Rossi's compositional method is both logical and analogical, translatable and untranslatable and, notwithstanding his declarations and his never-forsaken sympathies for rationalism, he does not deny the basic ambiguity in his work, in this sense rather like Venturi's. He himself has said: "A rational theory of art need not limit the meaning of the work to be built; since, if we know what we meant, and it is clear, we do not know what else was meant."

For Rossi, however, analogy is more than a tool for pervading his images with mnemonic references and unconscious meanings. It is also tied to typology and becomes a means for understanding and building the urban reality. This can be seen in Rossi's comments on the famous paintng which suggested to him the development of his theory:

Canaletto's view of Venice, now in the Parma Museum, seems to me to be the best clue for understanding the world of Venetian architecture in the Enlightenment . . . In the painting, the Rialto bridge, Palladian in design, the basilica and the Chiericati palace are all brought near and described as though the painter had rendered in perspective an urban environment which he had observed. And so the three Palladian monuments, of which one is a project, with elements which are both clear and tied to the history of both architecture and the city. The geographic transportation of the monuments around the project forms a city which we know, yet adapts it into a place of pure architectural significance.
The analogical Venice which comes into being is real and necessary; let's contribute to this logical-formal procedure, to this speculation about monuments and the disconcerting urban character in the history of art and of thought. A collage of Ralladian architecture forms a new city and in the act of doing so, reforms itself.

Along the lines of analogy, which, (as Brusatin has correctly noted), Lodoli already considered, along with solidity and comfort, "an essential property of representation," Rossi proposes a relationship between monument and city, between a part and the whole of the urban organism. This is a relationship that reaffirms Alberti's theory of the house as a small city and the city as a large house, confirming the humanistic roots of his thought.

Rossi's writings give another essential interpretive key in his discussion of the relationship between architecture and life in terms of reciprocal irreducibility. On the other hand, how can one explain the obvious contrast between the "warm humanity" of Rossi's personality and the impassive "coldness" of his works? He is profoundly convinced that an architecture which attempts to interact with and involve life must, in the final analysis, constrain it and limit its freedom.

He has written of the school by Fagnano Olona:

Within the spaces defined by architecture, the child's fantasy is free to build its own space, relating to its own personality without being conditioned by forms and methods which are alien to its experience, and therefore annoying. Often the presumed fantasy and irregularity of projects is only disorder; as such they should be dispensed with, principally in the case of public buildings.

A rigid world with few objects, therefore, which does not attempt to involve men, provoking their passions, but which in the course of life offer a fixed reference, like the surface of a mirror which can be animated at any moment by the warmth of the images it has generated. This is, for Rossi, the secret of Classicism, the attribute which allows buildings like the Pantheon, relating to the daily passage of the sun, to become measuring tools, gnomic indicators of time:

With this temporality, unveiled by light, classical architecture, born from an a priori idea, completely enclosed in a geometric thought, returns to a natural state; indeed, it will take on the meaning of a natural thing, fixed in time but perceived in the light of time. No organic adaption of forms can achieve this.

Classicism, then, not as a removal from life and from time, but as something existing in time. Light as "universal light," (which, in his control of materials, Rossi manages to capture in distinctive fashion), is therefore the last, faint testimony, (but also the only true one), to a sympathetic relationship between man and things, between architecture and its users.

He has written of the Trieste Regional Hall:

The same light and wind which transform the boys playing soccer and which mix together suburb and monument in the moments portrayed in the halted cities of Umberto Saba, in the background for every piece of architecture in Trieste. Saba's Trieste, a city parallel and inextricably bound to a love story, is stronger than any architecture; and so, this project is sited on a piece of Trieste, on the foundations of chipped stone which follow the river bank, as if on a broken shell. Looking for a physical relationship with the city, one which is direct and elementary, one finds it in the projection of the sky above the large glassed-in roofs. The moving sky, the wind, the rain, are buffetted about and reflect each other, seeking, like boats come into port, to momentarily capture the warm life of the city.

We have said from the beginning that Rossi removed himself from neo-rationalist equivocations. Although he has made certain statements openly expressing faith in the ahistorical continuity of the "architecture of reason," his detachment from the redeeming, utopian visions of the Modern Movement is so pronounced that it outweighs any statements to the contrary. The force and quality of Rossi's images, above all in his most important work, like the Scandicci project, the Modena cemetary and the "Teatro del Mondo", lie in his having set up an interaction among elements from the rationalist lexicon and the incessant flow of natural and artificial images arising from creative memory, expecting to extract permanent rules for the establishment of a convenient, reassuring "movement," have both misunderstood Rossi's ideas and have produced undistinguished results themselves.

Around 1964, shortly after the first student protests within the Italian architecture faculties, the Roman Group of Architects and Planners (GRAU) was formed. It was probably the first group of Italian architects to clearly and unequivocally disassociate itself from the Modern Movement. GRAU's proposals were somewhat more radical than those of the proponents of neo-realism and Neo-Liberty. The frame of reference they chose for criticizing the "tradition of the new," was not architecture's complex and contradictory reality, but rather its tradition, particularly, the line of development which tied together "classical" statements in western culture.

This attitude was openly at odds with the dominant view, but GRAU was driven by a series of strong beliefs and actual experiences which can be summarized as follows: 1) The belief that, along with neo-classical and eclectic precedents, modern architecture was part of a cycle of "architecture of the bourgeoisie," derived from an Marxist interpretation of the evolution of the Modern Movement; 2) A re-evaluation of the concept of art, shorn of late-romantic connotations and judged by historical-materialist interpretations, as indicated by the philosophy espoused by Galvano Della Volpe in his *Critique of Taste;* the architectural experience of Louis Kahn and the self-critical revisions of the leaders of modern architecture, demonstrated in some of their works in the 1950s.

These premises undermined the accepted truths which had prevailed in the post-war architecture world, and it was inevitable that they would be clearly refuted by certain central figures, such as Zevi, Benevolo, Quaroni, etc. But an unexpected and annoying reaction was the architecture world's feigned indifference, pushing GRAU into a sort of clandestine existence for years. This led to a slight adaptation of their philosophy, namely that architecture's renewal required not noisy statements and declarations of principle, but a slow, gradual and patient investigation and reconstruction, arising out of the "eternal present," that is, the history of architecture, seen as a totality of acknowledged achievement imbued with universal meaning.

More than ten years later, GRAU's accomplishments, first underground, then evermore open, are considerable, while the crumbling of modernist orthodoxy has invalidated the accusations and isolating strategies of GRAU's detractors. It has also become clear that GRAU's approach relates, or parallels, other situations in other cultural contexts, and in some cases GRAU has been the direct source of influence.

The dialectical unity of GRAU's projects, as well as their rediscovered "organic complexity," give the work its identity and significance, authoritatively placing it among the most advanced proponents of post-modernism. Granting certain differences which allow one to appreciate the creative presence of certain individuals within the group, all of GRAU's buildings and projects have a sense of process which is not additive and combinatory, but organic. The term organic is used here in the way that Della Volpe would advocate, but it also related directly to Alberti's "harmony," to Palladio and to Vasari's observations that he would describe Peruzzi's Farnesina as "not built, but born."

GRAU was faced with the spread of simplistic

espousals of the use of elementary solids from Euclidian geometry as primary and archetypal forms, as architectural matrices which could lead on back to the mental act of composition. They reacted by proposing another method by which forms are not objects to be simply arranged, but to be intersected, interpenetrated, metamorphosized through reciprocal relationships. Faced with the idea of mechanical juxtaposition, GRAU proposed a process of growth, whereby different forms are described, observed in their growth process and their reciprocal conditioning and the simultaneous obedience to and creation of common laws. They apply the lessons of Renaissance architecture without resorting to sterile revivalism, making possible, with renewed linguistic tools, a new investigation of ideas of "centrality," "translation," and the reciprocal attraction of volumetric unities.

As far as a critical approach to history, the Italian panorama, (other than the interrupted statements by the great masters, and the work of Rossi and GRAU), is rather bleak and characterized by a love-hate relationship toward the Modern Movement. This is surprising when one considers that after the second world war Italy was the country which published the greatest number of architectural histories, as well as the strongest ideological statements directed to the reconstruction of architectural history after the industrial revolution. A sort of guilt complex about the Modern Movement's confrontation with Fascism, (mystically inflating the Movement's charisma), has slowed down, even among younger generations, the process of detachment from the "tradition of the new," based on a Manichean division between progress and reaction.

And so the greatest efforts of the generation of architects who experienced the political upheavals of 1968 have been concentrated in the so-called tendenza. This relatively tight front has the distinction of having opened up the universities in reaction to the dominent, drab professionals who were in control. The "tendenza," however, has produced work of notable sterility, mixing together elements from Rossi's poetics, from Carlo Aymonino's fruitful examination of the relationship between typology and morphology and from Vittorio Gregotti's wide ranging ideas on architecture and place.

Nino Dardi can be singled out as fundamentally different from other adherents to the "tendenza." For years he concentrated on an investigation of an elementary lexicon based on the contradiction of closed and open forms and linear and central structures, knowledgeably filtered through their historical sources. Sandro De Feo also stands out, as one of the first to experiment with the professional ramifications of the Kahnian lexicon.

Purini was influenced by this movement, but never really a part of it. Among the most talented members of the architectural generation of the 1940s, he is known for his virtuoso drawings and his advocacy of "self described" architecture, whereby a finished object contains all the traces of the design process. After a successful collaborative period with Sacripanti and Gregotti, Purini applied himself to the development of a vocabulary which, from a distance, made it possible to identify the individual contributions to a project on the part of the various collaborators. This was achieved, on the other hand, through a survey approach, a description of elementary architectural situations by reassembling the components in additive fashion, like monads suspended from and orthogonal web. On the other hand, and more revealing in terms of Purini's relationship to history, he

has sought to recodify the images of an encounter/ confrontation between place and architecture, usually finding resolutions of surprising exactness. Purini has moved in the direction of mnemonic themes, as seen in his recent group of drawings dedicated to the "Roman house" (F. Purini, *Some Forms of the House*, Kappa, Rome, 1979), and in his extremely successful project for the facade of "Via Novissima," designed for the achitecture section of the Venice Biennial in July, 1980. In the latter project he breaks, for the first time, with his geometric universe and allows for the presence of precious and evocative scoria.

The architectural situation in Spain is similar to that in Italy—the scattered results of a rather mannered Neo-Realism hang on, after a timid period of experimentation in the early 1960s, which was then slowly abandoned in the wake of cultural demands and easy professional opportunities. While Rossi's example had nurtured both useful investigations of urban structures and sterile model-like exercises, Venturi's thoughts have provoked certain relevant and ironical architectural statements, among which is the particularly noteworthy "Georgina Belvedere" by Lluis Clotet and Oscar Tusquets. They also have designed a house on Pantelleria where the architecture subtly responds to the local landscape and agricultural culture. The Georgina Belvedere lies within the ironical tradition of garden pavilions and has the air of something either not quite finished or in a state of ruin, like "Le Desert" in Retz, built in 1771 by the knight, Racine de Monville. The recycling of traditional forms in the Georgina Belvedere allows the designers to both clarify their compositional method and to obtain a fascinating play of contrasting scales, inseparable from historical references to the templar system.

In Spain, however, the design team which has been most obvious in their break with the Modern Movement is the famous "Taller de arquitectura" in Barcellona. This group is composed of not only architects like Ricardo and Anna Bofill, but also philosophers, sociologists and scholars. Bolfill had already drawn attention to himself in 1968 with his Xanadu project, built on a rocky coast of Calpe. An enigmatic apartment house, pyramidal in form, results from the assembly (only apparently disorganized) of pieces which are derived from the current vocabulary of mediterranean building types. Xanadu appeared strange and irritating to many critics at the time, but over the past ten years the work of the Taller has become widely esteemed and accepted. Henri Lefebvre, one of the intellectuals active in the May 1968 protests at the University of Nanterre, has noted that Bolfill's work faces one of the most pressing problems in architecture today—the exploration of urban space. Unlike projects which "lose themselves in their enormity . . . attempting a compromise between monument and building," or those which "destroy the social space in their ephemeral unity and the flux of daily life," Bolfill's work (according to Bolfill) is closer to "what one should be thinking about and planning," pieces of cities which respond to needs which are generally disregarded: "the need for social life and for a center, the need and function for play, the symbolic function of space: needs and functions which go beyond those which are usually classified and dealt with rhetorically, which the poets call by the name desire."

Although the relationship with place and the use of historic memory proposed by the Taller seem to proceed more from unconscious suggestions, in the avant-garde tradition, their work undoubtedly achieves successful collective communication and environmental significance because of the strength and scope of their images. Their work has the character of an investigation, albeit fragmentary, of the prospects for a new urban environment and the restitution of symbolic value to architectural form. This is different from, but analogous to, the American espousal of banality in the urban environment, although the Taller dwells on an acceptance of society as it is, with its imperfections and vices, definitively abandoning any thought of preaching. José Augustin Goytisolo has written:

Every street, every quarter, every village, every city will have a new luminous and tranquil face, in accord with the vices and tastes of its inhabitants. It will be necessary to transfor today's housing blocks into offices of punishment or prisons for the architects and the speculators who commissioned them.

In Germany, a "recourse to memory" has slowly made its way, building on the ashes of one of the most sterile and insignificant offshoots of the International Style, the amorphous and alienating "German Reconstruction." Ungers and Gottfried Böhm were among the first to attempt architecture which connected back to regional culture, the former with an impassioned study of the work of Schinkel and his relationship with Berlin, the latter with a backwards journey, through expressionism, toward the structural components of the "romantic" urban landscape.

In Austria during the last decade, the work of Hans Hollein stands out. During the 1960s he designed interiors which were noteworthy for both their rigor and their surprising immaginative force, inaugurating an entire genre based on contrasts between the purity of the container and the unpredictability of the symbolic and plastic themes which distort the surrounding homogeneity.

Hollein continued with more complex and significant orchestrations of his ideas, culminating in the interiors for the offices of a travel agency in Vienna, where natural and historical citations, transformed by their realization in unusual materials, neither generates eclectic confusion nor plays itself out like a sequence of travel posters evoking touristic sites. The objects Hollein has chosen—a column, palms, an Indian kiosk—are semantic poles around which he constructs a pleasurable space which the neutral envelope of the walls refuses to define.

England occupies a key position in the so-called "Post-Modern" experience, due not only to the important contribution of James Stirling, which, from 1969 on, exhibit a troubled but intense attempt to deal with the poetics of memory, but also to the propagandistic and didactic activities of Charles Jencks, and from 1969 onwards to the presence of Leon Krier. James Stirling was the greatest exponent of Neo-Brutalism, and his famous polemical statement in 1956—"Let's face it, William Morris was a Swede"—shows his determined opposition to any architecture which might have connotations of the English traditionalism. According to his point of view, a regression toward regionalism is a great disaster to be avoided at all costs. For this reason, perhaps, his relationship with history never takes the form of an aggressive renunciation of the Modern Movement. This relationship is evident in his treatment of the surfaces of the large volumes of the "social valley" designed for the Siemens complex, (where Krier's contribution is also apparent), and in his placement of the old facade of the Asembly Hall at a 30° incline—a deliberately implacable recomposition within the context of the Derby civic center. Throughout the 1970s, Stirling's work systematically reproposed—in a manner which always had the benefit of his great professional "bravura"—both an attraction to and a fear of mnemonic themes. This, however, never becomes the main condition in his work.

In the early 1970s, the presence of Leon Krier in Stirling studio seemed to indicate a turn in direction, but in no way lessened his empirical vacillations or his evasive, rather than structural, use of irony. The logical consequences of certain works from this period are therefore found not so much in Stirling's own work, but in the autonomous work of Leon Krier.

The work of Leon Krier, born in Luxembourg in 1946, is inextricably linked to that of his brother, Rob, born in 1938. First of all, the Krier brothers entertain a common passion for the European city all with its historical ramifications, prior to the disintegration introduced by an analytical approach to modern planning. Their idea of city is expressed in a continuum, the primary elements of which are the street and the piazza, with respect to which historic monuments function as points of reference. Rob Krier has written.

The fascination that the historical centers of our cities hold for us lies in their almost indeterminable variety of forms assumed by the urban space with its corresponding architecture. Every epoch has, in its way, extended its technical capability, be this the development of the picture frame or massive stone or brick construction. Thanks to this, architecture has never had to compromise in terms of quality. To the contrary! The wealth of forms comes principally from the fact that architects never abandoned their control over their work, but commanded sufficient time to study and elaborate the elements of construction—often extremely complicated—and also that the client understood and required architecture as an art form. One used to know how to build in the city and, conversely, how to build in the country. In the city, architecture had to establish a dialogue with its historical substance, and not, as happens today, to remove itself from all its fundamental structures in favor of an extistence which is solitary and hostile to any integration. Every new urban plan must adapt itself to the order of the total structure, and its form must correspond to that which already exists.

From this theory, Rob Krier has derived a sort of abacus of spatial situations which constitutes one of the most lucid attempts to understand the historical inheritance of western urban civilization. His projects then employ this abacus in various situations, working within the design of the existing city to reweave the actual fabric, or to insert autonomous spatial elements. His architectural vocabulary, however, rarely frees itself from reductive games of cut-out voids placed against surfaces modelled on white, Loosian skeletons.

The architecture and planning projects of Leon Krier faithfully interpret the same program for reintegrating the urban environment. In Leon's work, however, other polemical motives also play a role, such as a reclamation of the "pleasure of architecture" and a bond to political struggle. He has written:

It is necessary to recognize that, in the realm of social divisions of work, the pursuit of pleasure is denied, not only in manual labor but also in its intellectual counterpart. My principal concern is not to elaborate a personal language or to simulate a new style; rather, I am interested in to rediscovery of a constructive logic, in a popular culture, in the genius of a collective language where the form is the *intelligent* result of a dignified manual production.

And, apropos the significance of this reintegration, he adds:

The reconstruction of the public dimension and of an architecture which is capable of expressing it must become the principal goal of a progressive and democratic political struggle, for the simple fact that this cannot be a mechanical result.

The simple clarity, and exaggerated paradoxical tone of the Krier brothers' statements, (especially those of Leon), have certainly contributed to their didactic success, but their position risks an "archeologization" of the city. There is a contradiction in their work between a proposition for a complex and articulated urban space and the use of an architectural language which is lacking in complexity and meager in its conventions, deduced in part, though theoretically distant from, the work of Aldo Rossi.

Along these lines, references to history risk repeating the mistakes of the Modern Movement which were based on the illusion that society could be changed through architecture and planning. This is precisely the fate of the in many ways interesting work of the Le Cambre school under the direction of Maurice Culot, who explicitly refers to the Kriers' theories. At La Cambre, the critiques of both Le Corbusier's *The Athens Charter* and the principles of building speculation raise the banner of "anti-industrial resistence" and align the school with the community struggles in Brussels. A strange mix of Marxist motives and the utopian socialism of Morris, (completely forgetting the Marxist thesis of the function of industrial development as a midwife of the revolution) are used to justify a disciplinary program which entails a return to an imitation of archetypes which, in fact, are drawn from the theoretical teachings of the *bourgeoise* revolution: Ledoux and Boullée, primarily. This fragile theoretical basis in part counteracts the fervor and enthusiasm which animates Culot's group, which has produced projects which have the ingenuous charm of a new Biedermayer.

At the beginning of the 1960s, the French architectural world seemed the most acritically accepting of modernist orthodoxy and the furthest from the lively ferment already taking place in Italy and in the United States. The political viewpoint of the magazines, the academic world's stance and the predilection of the building industry for enormous, all-encompassing projects all contributed to a prevailing conformity and mediocrity. Thus the equation predicted by Mies in the 1920s—architecture = construction—was realized, but reduced to an act of pure will at the expense of quality.

Le Corbusier's death in 1965 deprived this desolate scene of its undeserved claim to glory, the presence of an international leader, recognized but not accepted. His teachings, always at odds with the official academic establishment, were never really incorporated and bore only sporadic and disappointing fruits. Le Corbusier's legacy, mediated by Candilis or the Atelier d'Urbanisme et d'Architecture, will undoubtedly represent one of the strong points of French achievements of this period, within the limitations, however, of the philosophy that "planning" can be isolated from architecture and can be substituted for it in a technological society. The results have been negligible in terms of the cultural renewal of the city.

The events of 1968 threatened the establishment's balance and, although numerous equivocal stands were taken, there was a major shifting of priorities.

Bernard Huet and his group, (begun in 1965 under the name "Collegiale I"), have the clear distinction of having introduced to France the provocative architectural issues being debated in Italy—urban analyses; the relationship between typology and morphology; the legacy of Louis Kahn, (with whom Huet had studied); the theoretical arguments of Team X. In 1974 Huet was made the editor-in-chief of *Architecture d'Aujourd'Hui*, the magazine which was the symbol of the French architectural establishment, and it suddenly appeared that a battle had been won. In fact, the greatest battles were still to be fought, as can be seen in his dismissal from the magazine in 1977.

Fernando Montes has written that "The Liberation was a lost historic opportunity for transforming French architecture." May 1968 will be seen as another quest for a convergence between politics and architecture. On December 6, 1968, six months following the first upheavals, a decree was published which signalled the death of ENSBA, the Ecole Nationale Superieur des Beaux-Arts. Two years later, Max Querrie, director of architecture at the Ministry of Culture, formed a commission on reform, composed of professors, students and officials. May '68 had accelerated all this activity, and the application of reforms was inevitable. In 1962 another anticipated official reform was virtually abrogated, but finally the ancient cultural grande-dame, more feudal now than matriarchal, was put out to pasture and replaced by the U.P.—the "Pedagogical Unity for Architecture"—an educationally and administratively autonomous entity.

It is paradoxical that precisely at that moment when the architectural world elsewhere, and particularly in America, was re-evaluating the Beaux-Arts teachings, the old institution, which had long ago lost its identity, definitively gave up its central position in France and become one of many minor, independent alternatives. The result was a pluralistic but confused horizon, initially dominated by many of the myths inherited or cultivated by the 1968 student movement: multidisciplinariness, a homology of architecture and politics, the scientific approach, professionalism.

During the decade which followed, there slowly emerged out of this heterogeneous and discordant panorama, a resolute approach, capable of confronting problems with a specifically architectural vocabulary, an approach which looked to history as a tool for acknowledging, understanding and reproducing urban phenomena.

From the beginning, this consciously historicist orientation characterized the work of certain French academic institutions. Attitudes which initially espoused the absolute primacy of politics and the futility of disciplinary engagement gradually changed to attitudes which recognized the significance of research, at least in the "pure" dimension of design.

From 1969 to 1972 one group consisted in part of architects like Grumbach, Lion, Lucan, Montes and Portzamparc. Olivier Girard has written that their tendency was

... to refute any possibility of architectural production, which they considered in any case to be pure self-satisfaction, an illusory hope and above all a hypocritical concealment of the true class role of the architect of every so-called competent architectural product. But this subgroup, while participating in the organization of UP6 as a militant seat of denunciation of the politics of housing and the alienation of urban renewal, nevertheless allowed for the possibility of designed and therefore cultural interventions which could be consistent with their militancy. Above all, they

disavowed a return to institutionalization of architectural education, imposed by the Ministry, which forced them to exclude the idea of any architectural curriculum in the schools. Shortly thereafter, the creation and diffusion of the newspaper, "What do we want: Everything," signalled their passage out of a "self-castrating," self-denying and hating phase. Their interest then turned to the psychoanalysis of Lacan, reawakening a "desire for city" as "the space of desire," a sense of history as the unconscious, the design as discourse, place as a moment of binomial differentiation—segregation.

And so, having passed the "self-castrating" phase, the architects of this group, together with others like Girard Laisnay Paurd, the TAU group (consisting of Huet, Bigelman, Feugas, Le Roy and Santelli), assumed an increasingly consistent role in the search for an alternative to the Modern Movement. Their achievements are notable for their quality and also benefit from comparison with the prevailing attitudes toward both a reintegration of urban values and a reclamation of architectural knowledge endowed with autonomy and specificity.

The architect who as most thoroughly expressed an original vision, despite his extreme youth, is Christian de Portzamparc, from Brittany. He is the designer of the rue des Hautes Formes and of the Marne-la Vallé water towers, both of which have contributed to a world-wide awareness of a revival of a typically French style on an urban scale.

Portzamparc had already captured the public's eye in 1974 with a design notable for its imaginative power and its rigorous formal discipline—his entry for the competition for Le Roquette island. A large, enclosed space is surrounded by a continuous succession paired niches, alternated with tall portals. He obtains a gigantic architectural order without resorting to columns or cornices, but by the adoption of building volumes as elements of an elementary code of immediate effectiveness. At the time Portzamparc wrote:

Between morphology and typology, the scale of the order imposes a space which is no longer seen as the sole result or a conclusion of urban and technical chains, of programs or intentional functions; another logic, intrinsic to the project, develops out of the technical or aesthetic unity of the architectural object, to generate a space which is first of all a public urban space and, in the tension between nature and habitat, a spatial symbol of the entire city.

Portzamparc's rue des Hautes Formes adheres to this same line and is a demonstration that the program of a rediscovered urbanity is not a utopian program which requires abnormal typologies and production costs beyond the scope of public projects. He proposes, along with skillfully designed apartments which conform to prevailing standards, some interesting internal spatial solutions, without, moreover, exceeding standard building costs. He has demonstrated, in overwhelming fashion, that prefabrication—as it is employed in France, without the generic brutality typical of Italian examples, which rarely break out of the obsolete "tunnel" system—does not preclude a limited shaping of the urban environment or the attainment of variety and freedom in the design of both volumes and open spaces.

The Marne-la-Vallée water tower has a similar figurative impact, with its spiralling shape inspired by the typology of the Tower of Babel, mediated by Boullée. It constitutes an unpredictable and magical urban event in the midst of a wooded square at the entrance to a chaotic new town which, unfortunately, has little else to offer but, at least in this case, seems to indicate the visual pleasure and the provocation of desire as a possible antidote to chaos and boredom, The tower, sheathed in a transparent grill which supports the climbing plants which grow around the volume, is truly a "castle" (in the French sense of the word) for the water which, hidden from view, inhabits the top portion and descends to the interior by invisible passageways. Portzamparc has evidently tried to overturn the much-used theme of the generator which rests, like a tank on a slender shaft. According to Georgia Benamo:

This distortion of use, function, scale, symbol, languages and signs produces something unpredictable which is pure joy. This exhaustion of the culture is new: there is a Tower of Babel, but it is culturally destroyed, veiled, covered up, fortunate. The old myth has been turned around: the different languages coexist, working side by side without destroying themselves.

In his project for the Trou des Halles, recently exhibited in Florence, Portzamparc reproposes within a public space the rhythmic arrangement of buildings with which he had experimented in his La Roquette project. Here he uses a more tightly knit arrangement, but it is always accompanied by an extraordinary sense of proportion. Large windows and small openings alternate in a manner which seems to confer a recognizable physiognomy to the surfaces, giving almost the impression of a human face. And so here, too, his architecture becomes figurative.

Coming out of the political extremism of the early 1970s, which carried with it moralistic renunciations of the discipline, Fernando Montes formulated an approach, timid but coherent, based on the assemblage of forms which seem familiar, "already seen." Classicism is his guiding idea, but not a classicism which is taken for granted or reduced to a style, but a classicism which reveals itself in a sense of balance, in a relationship between neighboring or superimposed objects, which is always a complementary relationship and one of reciprocal desire. In this universe of forms, large and small things, fundamental or accessory, are all indispensible. The obelisque, the spire, the porthole are never "ornament" because their "weight" is necessary for the scales to balance; the negative forces are equivalent to the positive ones. Montes arrived in France from his homeland with the intention of finding one of the designated lands of great architecture and, probably disappointed with the impoverished present, he did not hesitate to look for guidance outside his own time, among the ranks of the "revolutionaries," where the rule of reason asserts its permanent and abstract laws.

Montes has proposed an institute of semiology, dedicated to Roland Barthes, in which Palladio and Ledoux join forces and seem to merge with Aldo Rossi and Leon Krier in the celebration of archetypes. Here, the intellectual game, played with an open hand, prevails over any analysis of real space, although on other occasions Montes has shown that he can descend without stumbling from the stage of symbolical design, applying himself to productive terrain. This is certainly the case in his housing complex at Cergy-Pontoise, a large circular piazza surrounded by houses crossed by large arched openings—one of the most successful applications of the idea of the large urban court, reproposing in new terms the theme of the Palais Royal.

For his counter-project for Les Halles, Montes is among the few architects to have taken into account the presence of the church of Saint Eustache. He sets it within a U-shaped space, with the open end facing the side of the sixteenth century building. This solution is based entirely on a play of influences and a correspondence between the new and old sections of the city which takes on the persuasive tone of a dialogue.

Antoine Grumbach's work is particularly interesting in terms of his reclamation of urban parks. One of his fundamental propositions, as seen in the exhibition, *Roma interrotta*, is an inverse, vegetative archeology which poetically interprets the theme of conservation and the utilization of cultural goods.

At the end of this book, which has sought to grasp an overall pattern, gathering together separate fragments of a mosaic which only the passage of time will allow to be correctly deciphered, the reader may well ask, like the figures in a famous painting by Gauguin: "Where do we come from? Who are we? Where are we going?". The historian's goal is to demonstrate the facts and to establish the relationships among the facts which express a cause and effect chain. But the goal of one who is still in the midst of events is, rather, to persuade and to involve others. And, in fact, these pages have the sense of an invitation, addressed not only to young novices, but to all possible readers, so as to allow them to be engaged by this great wave which has swept modern architecture back into the fold of history, removing it from its pedestal.

Even recently, certain historians have sought to explain the phenomena discussed here by reproposing the rather stale label, "avant-garde," thereby showing that they have not understood that, if, indeed, the masquerading avant-gardist still holds some fascination for certain marginal exponents of post-modernism, that fascination for certain marginal exponents of post-modernism, that fascination is really nothing more than a nostalgic reference. The true Copernican revolution has not been designed at the drafting table, but is a product of the new conditions on transmission and production in the post-modern world. This revolution consists of the pulling down of the dike between the present and the past, and, the mixing of the waters from both has intensified the push toward the future—a future where we will be, in Jencks' appropriate phrase, "the primitives of a new sensibility."

There is no hurry, then to disclose the figure which time will reveal, filling in the missing fragments of the unfinished mosaic. These pages do not indicate certainties, but paths by which, holding to the principle of doubt, one might possibly grasp fragments of truth.

As is often the case with phenomena in their nascent state, architecture which has emerged from new relationships has a temporary and at times precarious nature which makes it more meaningful in terms of what it lays the ground for than what it actually is. Can it make sense, at this point, to speak of a new renaissance, even if the phrase is tied to the thesis of an Italian sociologist? The term "renaissance" is too linked to a specific historic past to appear useful and unequivocal. In any case, it is worthwhile to reclaim the concept of a "return to the old" which, given the cyclical nature of certain phenomena, is extremely appropriate to the current, still unfolding, state of affairs.

Eugenio Battisti has written in the *Universal Encyclopedia of Art*:

The return to the old is an attitude which is not identified with the occasional or the personal inclination, dependent upon the psychology of individual artists . . . nor can it be taken as a moment in the normal process of artistic development or as an interval or meditative lull after a period of intense activity; nor should it be seen as a more or less latent form of conservatism with respect to current tastes . . . it should, however, really be understood as a positive turn, a revival of problems which presumably cannot be resolved with material from the present, immediate tradition . . . Therefore, the return to the old should be distinguished, first of all, from tradition and, in a certain sense, is its opposite.

Battisti's lucidly theoretical definition, proposed in an unsuspecting era, is echoed by the explicit statements of many architects mentioned here who have reclaimed their right to react against the "modern" tradition, just as the protagonists of the avant-garde reacted against the eclectic tradition.

The valiant defenders of the recent past adopt as a last resort the thesis that we risk throwing away a patrimony which might still yield worthwhile results. This is unconvincing on at least two accounts. First, this extreme caution and conservatism betrays one of the few indisputably strong attributes of the Modern Movement, namely its intellectual courage. The second point is that no generation which possesses a minimum of creativity could prescribe living off a marginal, meager patrimony which is on its way to extinction.

The only possible use for the great spiritual adventure, modern architecture, is to function like the ladder of Wittgenstein. It can be used to look, from above, at everything which lies around and in back, but it must then be thrown away, immediately and without regrets since, although it was indispensible for climbing up, once the destination has been reached it becomes a useless hindrance.

What is certain, however, is that we see both the past and the present through the lens of modern architecture. Its tradition permeates our minds and our eyes. The true dilemma is whether to use this legacy to go forward or to leave it to rot on the shelves like the wartime hoarders who saw their accumulated supplies change in two possible ways: either into swarming worms or into moths which flew away.

These phenomena which we have illustrated and summarized have already been the object of diverse studies and interpretations. Some of these have been analyzed here, others have been skipped over since they were outside the scope of this book. In particular it has not been deemed opportune to examine those interpretations which tend to define the present situation in architecture as a dead-end street, an endeavor doomed to failure without the intervention of a providential *deus ex machina*, be it a revolution or the death or our civilization. We are instinctively suspicious of that line of thought, with its myths and rites of negation in which, as psychoanalysis has taught us, we can recognize personal and suprapersonal motivations and traits.

All interpretations of the post-modern condition, be they pessimistic or optimistic, confront a changed world which demands attempts at comprehension and attention, before judgments are passed. The task of establishing whether this world is better or worse than those which preceeded it cannot be accurately fulfilled at this short distance. In any case, all too often those who presume to have made such judgment have chosen as their point of comparison some imprecise golden age, or a society idealized for certain qualities which have been arbitrarily extrapolated from the overall picture. The transformation of a society and a culture implies the modification of the roles played by both individuals and groups, often with "high" places exchanged for more modest ones. It is understandable, but not justifiable, that the affected categories will identify their loss of importance with wide-spread cultural decadence. The changes in stature of a certain discipline signify the end of a world, not the end of the world.

The post-modern world heralds the collapse and the unfeasability of the grand, centralized systems with which one once attempted to explain everything. Lyotard has written:

Let us pay attention to that which is not resolvable, to the limits of accurate verification, to the conflicts arising from incomplete information, to disjunctures, to catastrophes, to pragmatic paradoxes with which post-modern science formulates the true theory of evolution as something discontinuous, catastrophic, non-correctable, paradoxical. Post-modernism changes the meaning of the verb "to know," and it tells how this change will take place. It produces not the known but the unknown. And it suggests a model for legitimization which is by no means based on the greatest yield, but rather based on differences understood as paralogisms.

This apparent disorientation will be disappointing for those who would like to see a return to the days when intellectuals, as Toqueville says, had become "the most important political men of their time," the only important ones, since even if others exercised power, the intellectuals appeared to be "the only ones endowed with authority." But this role, established during the Enlightenment, has changed over time and has been turned over to many others. The new roles of authority are played by the data banks which exceed the capacity of any user and make possible elaborations of complete bodies of information. With these new "authorities" one must know, above all, how to establish untried and unpredictable connections among series of facts, resorting to a sort of combinatory fantasy and a game of reciprocal influences.

It may be that ours is a time of ephemeral beliefs, in which images are reduced to "semblances," copies without originals—a time when culture is no longer a double for reality. But this world, in other ways, might be diagnosed in the opposite fashion. Mario Perniola has written:

Culture has always thought of itself as a *double*, with respect to reality, both as a value system in opposition to the world, and as a tool for dominating it: it was sometimes distant, sometimes near, but always a double of reality. It is this duplicity which has failed. The gift which new times have brought to culture is the advent of a single dimension. If this monodimensionality has seemed a catastrophe to a traditional intellectual like Marcuse, it is because he has seen the phenomenon only from the point of view of values and has not understood that it also implies the ruin of the instrumental pragmatic perspective. On the other hand, this monodimentionality does not imply a homogenization or a general levelling of life, nor does it imply the end of the image; to the contrary, it implies a place where the image is indistinguishable from the real, where it, in fact, becomes a *simulacrum*. The simulacrum is not a pictorial image which reproduces an external prototype, but an effective image which dissolves the original. As in the Mohave Desert, where intentions remain sterile and ineffectual as long as they are not dreamed, so in contemporary society, the unqualified acceptance of the dimension of the simulacrum is the necessary condition for its effectiveness.

CONCLUSION

This book, and the exhibition at the Biennial *The Presence of the Past*, which in certain aspects constitutes its natural continuation on a practical level, have been at the center of a lively and impassioned debate, the likes of which has not taken place in the architectural world for many years. The tone of the debate has been at times bitter, at times calm, and it has frequently been dominated by the vulgarity of those who, failing to grasp the broad significance of a phenomenon, seek to reduce it to its most paradoxical and minor aspects, in order to combat it and thereby delude themselves into thinking that they have annihilated it.

There is, however, no lack of profound and committed contributions to this dispute on the future of architecture, and these deserve a thoughtful reply, for they have stimulated and enriched the debate. We dedicate this provisional conclusion to these contributions, and in particular to the text of Jurgen Habermas which was delivered on the occasion of the conferring of the Adorno prize. We will neglect to comment on, (but not to thank), those who have, on the other hand expressed their strong support for the theses espoused in the book and the exhibition.

Habermas writes:

The term "modern" was used for the first time in the late fifth century, to distinguish the Christian presence, which had then become official, from the pagan-Roman past. With changing contents, "modernity" will always express itself as the conscience of an epoch which presents itself in relation to the past of the ancients, seeing itself as the result of a passage from the old to the new.

This holds true, not only for the Renaissance, which is the beginning of the modern era for us, but for other epochs as well. The term "modern" was also applicable in the time of Charlemagne in the twelfth century, and during the Englightenment—every time, then, that people in Europe became conscious of a new epoch through a change in their relationship with the past. Along these lines, *antiquitas* is valid as a model which one is encouraged to imitate. Only with the ideals of the French Enlightenment, with its concept of infinite progress of consciousness, inspired by modern science and social and moral betterment, were the respective "moderns" freed from the constraints imposed by the classical, ancient world. Finally, the "modern" searches for its true past in an idealized Middle Ages, contrasting the romantic to the classical.

We will not follow Habermas in his entire reconstruction of the historic journey of "modernity," but we must at least point out the scant attention, (symptomatic, after all), paid to the Renaissance paradox of "rediscovered antiquity." In fact, in early Renaissance texts it is not unusual for the terms "modern" and "moderns" to refer not to the new culture, but to the old, that is, to the gothic culture which for many decades remained the dominent force to which humanist thought reacted. Before modernity could be identified with a revival of the norms of classical antiquity, it was necessary, in fact, to definitively conclude the battle against the waning modernity represented by the remnants of gothic internationalism. And a similar battle will occur two centuries later, for example, when Father Pozzo will defend his "modernity," in the Baroque era, from the homogenizing dogmas of the classicist critics who, a few decades later, would have found "progressive" support in the emerging culture of the Enlightenment. Without understanding the historic dialectic of modernity and without a philological verification of the alternation of values and meanings, the history of the word "modern" loses all substance and risks creating a non-existent fetish, homologous to the fictitious semantic stability.

Habermas' failure to deal with the dialectical nature of modernity and its many guises keeps him from seeing the circuitous nature of the path he has taken, which he seems, instead, to have reduced to a single, linear route. His method is necessary if he is to propose to us, in apparently convincing fashion, the equation that modernity = progress, from which the opposite is deducible—that anti-modernity or post-modernism = conservatism. And, in fact, in his initial discussion of the critics of modernism, Habermas cites only a spokesman of this persuasion—Daniel Bell, a self-proclaimed political and philosophical conservative. He thereby casts suspicion on anyone who points out the obsolescence of modernism.

In fact, my colleague, Daniel Bell, the most brilliant of the American neo-conservatives, thinks along these lines. In his book, *The Cultural Contradictions of Capitalism*, Bell defends the thesis that the crises of developed societies in the western world stem from a fracture between culture and society. Avant-garde art has penetrated the value scale of every day life, infecting the world of life *(Lebenswelt)* with the idea of modernism. This latter is the great seducer, which gives authority to the principle of unbridled self-realization, the quest for authentic experience and the subjectivity of an overstimulated sensitivity. In this way, hedonistic feelings are let loose which are incompatible with the discipline of professional life and in general with the principles of conduct of a rational-utilitarian life.

Bell thereby blames the disintegration of the Protestant ethic, which had already disturbed Max Weber, on the adversary culture, that is a culture which modernism had nurtured with hostility toward the conventions and the virtues of everyday life rationalized by the economy and the science of administration.

Habermas reduces criticisms of the modern tradition to these physiocratic lamentations, without giving any examples of a less generic nature. Noting the discomfort produced by a certain weariness of the "project of modernity," he seems to want to reduce his own argument to the celebrated apology of the baby and the bathtub water.

I am of the opinion that we would do better to be aware of the aberrations which have accompanied modernism's program and the errors of the presumptuous proposals for its overthrow, rather than giving up for lost modernism and its program.

As for the errors he mentions, however, he doesn't seem to have taken the trouble to know them well, because he avoids enumerating them and skips rapidly, instead, to a classification of the guilty according to three categories, or three measures of neo-conservatism—the young, the old and, finally, the "neo-conservatives" themselves:

The young conservatives assimilate the basic experience of the aesthetic model, the discovery of decentralized subjectivity, freed from all the imperatives of work and utility, and thereby escape from the modern world. With a modernist attitude, they define their own brand of intransigent anti-modernism. They cast off the spontaneous forces of the imagination, of true knowledge and feeling, to a distant and archaic realm, and in Manichean fashion they propose instead a principle which is open only to evocation of a desire for power, supremacy, existence, or a Dionysian poetic force. In France this line of thought runs from Bataille, to Foucault, up to Derrida.

The old-conservatives do not allow themselves, initially to have anything to do with modern culture. They follow, with distress, the decline of substantial reason, the differentiation progress of rationality, recommending a return to pre-modern conditions. Neo-Aristotelianism, above all, has met with a certain success, allowing the encouragement of cosmic explanations for ecological issues. Along this line of thought, stemming from Leo Strauss, there are, for example, interesting works by Hans Jonas and Robert Spaemann.

The neo-conservatives, finally, welcome the development of modern science, as long as it goes beyond its sphere only to accelerate technological progress, capitalistic creativity and rational administration. Apart from this, they recommend a policy which defuses the explosive content of cultural modernism.

One thesis declares that science, if properly understood, has become completely unimportant for an orientation in life. Another thesis says that politics must remain free from all demands of moral-practical justification. A third thesis insists on the pure immanence of art and negates its utopian content invoking its apparent disposition to isolate the aesthetic experience in private. One could point out the early middle and later periods of Gottfried Benn's work as examples.

The list is long, and no matter what one's predilection, it is likely that one would be in good company. But what still needs to be explained is now Habermas can use the unifying label "conservative" for positions which are so incompatible with and far from each other, while he denies the label to those who doubtlessly and in explicit fashion want to jealously conserve something: namely, the inconclusive program of "modernity." Why inconclusive? Why unfinished? And if the nature of modernity is truly its incapacity to conclude, why hasn't it taken into account that its meaning has continuously changed throughout history, making both its friends and enemies seem like ghost hunters.

It is truly disappointing that the Frankfurt school, after having supported the inexorable anxiety of Adorno, the most radical critic of consumerism and the obsolescence of "modernity," today expresses, through the defensive stance of Habermas, an attempt to hibernate, to withdraw from the harsh realities of a changed world.

Habermas unwittingly ends up giving credence to Schelsky, whose positivist conclusions he had sharply criticized in his *Logic of the Social Sciences.* He attributes the re-emergence of archetypes, of which the Venice exhibition has been the most obvious symptom, to a defeat of the avant-garde. Habermas seems, in fact, to underline Schlesky's affirmation of the "scientification of the past":

From the moment when the past, which traditionally prescribed a plan of action to both individuals and groups, was outdistanced by the historical sciences, an objective world was established, open to critical-scientific investigation. Modern man gains the freedom of an open future which, alone, can make him capable of transforming, according to scientific conceptions, the natural and the social environment. The "lack of historicity" of modern society, demonstrated through natural and social prodecures, has then, the scientification of the past as an assumed premise.

The illusion that our technological civilization can remove itself from history, the inanity of a withdrawal which has more often than not produced only alienation and violence, ought to convince us that it is time to abandon the myth of

Lot's wife, who was punished by God for having turned around to look behind her. It is the loss of memory, not the cult of memory, that will make us prisoners of the past.

Adorno was acutely aware of how one could be the unknowing victim of an inherited revolution, describing the drama of the second generation of modern composers as a dream of rootlessness.

The innovators, like Schönberg, Bartok, Stravinsky, Webern, Berg and also Hindemith, came to maturity completely within traditional music. Their language, their critical and contradictory spirit was consistent in its relationship with tradition, while those who came later no longer had this tradition alive within them and, instead, changed a musical ideal, critical of itself, into a falsely positive factor, without the necessary application of spontaneity or effort.

The Modern Movement in architecture has had the sad privilege of having remained for years a "falsely positive factor," losing all real capacity for renewal, precisely because, after the efforts of the first generations, its critical potential was exhausted, as well as its grand and contradictory, ephemeral nature with respect to the historical tradition. After the fruitful period of self-questioning, between the end of the last century and 1925—a period in which it is no accident that there is renewed interest—modernity imposed on architecture a rejection of language, which neither literature nor music would have been able to accept or practice with equal rigor. The reemergence of archetypes in all their complexity and contradictions, which this book has examined, is, then, not a jealous but a joyous rediscovery of something which was previously constrained to live clandestinely within us. This rediscovery can only help us to reduce the isolation of a discipline which in fifty years has progressively lost its specific function as a matrix of urban figurative art, on the one hand, and technological production without quality on the other.

In recent years the Japanese naval industry has produced some extremely modern ships which are strongly energy-efficient, thanks to a splendid and very complicated sail apparatus, controlled and maneuvered by an electronic mechanism. The architecture of post-industrial society will probably resemble these enchanted sailing ships.

PROSPETTO SUD

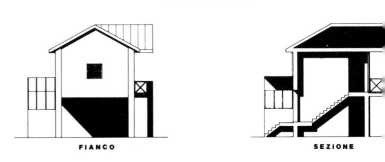

PROSPETTO NORD

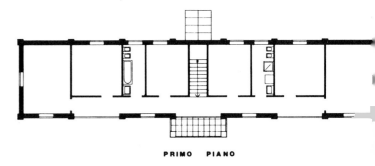

FIANCO   SEZIONE

*Aldo Rossi, competition project for Sannazzaro de'
Burgondi Piazza, 1967.*

*Aldo Rossi with A. Pizzigoni, residence, Bergamo, 1977,
(photograph by F. Moschini).*

PRIMO   PIANO

Aldo Rossi, project for apartment house, Zandobbio, 1979.

Aldo Rossi, project for houses along the Verbindungskanal, Berlin, 1976.

BELOW AND RIGHT:
Aldo Rossi with Aldo De Poli, Giulio Dubbini, Marino Narpozzi, perspective views of project in Cannareggio district, Venice, 1978.

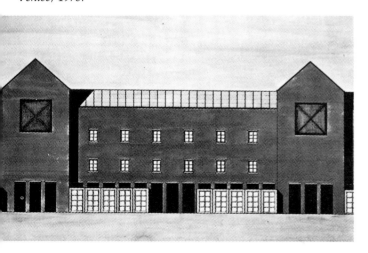

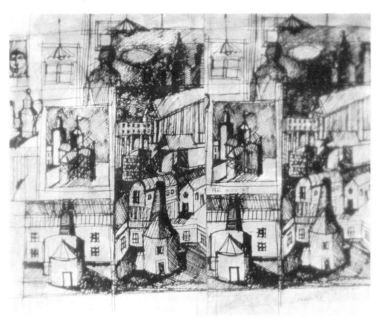

Aldo Rossi with G. Braghieri, drawing for Modena Cemetery, 1971–79.

Aldo Rossi, project for Trieste Regional Hall, 1974.

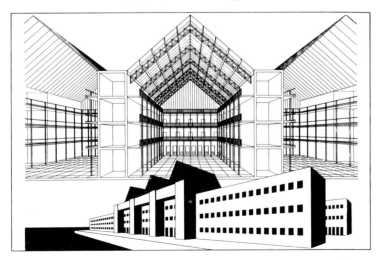

Aldo Rossi, "Teatro del Mondo," Venice, 1979.

115

Aldo Rossi, "Little Theater with the Hand of the Saint and Shadow," 1978.

Aldo Rossi, gateway, De Amicis School, Broni, 1970, (photograph by F. Moschini).

BELOW AND BELOW LEFT:
Aldo Rossi, middle school, Broni, 1980.

Alessandro Anselmi (GRAU), plan, project for Les Halles District, Paris, 1979.

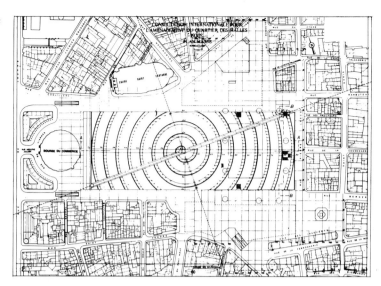

Luigi Pisciotti and Uberto Siola with G. Raimondino, exterior view, house, Maiori, Salerno, 1969.

. Anselmi, P. Chiatante, R. Mariotti, F. Pierluisi (GRAU), flower market, Sanremo (Imperia), perspective view of accessible rooftop first solution), 1973-75.

lessandro Anselmi with Giovanni De Sanctis, project for a nursery hool, Guidonia, 1965.

Luigi Pisciotti and Uberto Siola with G. Raimondino, plan, house, Maiori, Salerno, 1969.

Alessandro Anselmi and Paola Chiatante (GRAU), *perspective view, project for Les Halles District, Paris, 1979.*

M. Martini, P. Nicolosi (GRAU), with E. Rosati, Mastroianni *house, Rome, 1975, (photograph by F. Moschini).*

M. Martini, G.P. Patrizi (GRAU), with E. Rosati, Rosati *House, Rome, 1972.*

Franco Purini, "The Roman House," gallery house, ink drawing on tracing paper, 1979.

Franco Purini, "The Roman House," principal facade, ink drawing on cardboard, 1978.

Franco Purini, "After Modern Architecture," etching on zinc, 1977.

Bruno Reichlin and Fabio Reinhardt, central hall, Sartori House, Riveo, Ticino Canton, 1976–77.

Bruno Reichlin and Fabio Reinhardt, facade, Sartori House, Riveo, Ticino Canton, 1976–77.

Alessandro Anselmi and Paola Chiatante, (GRAU), Parabita Cemetery (Lecce), 1967–79.

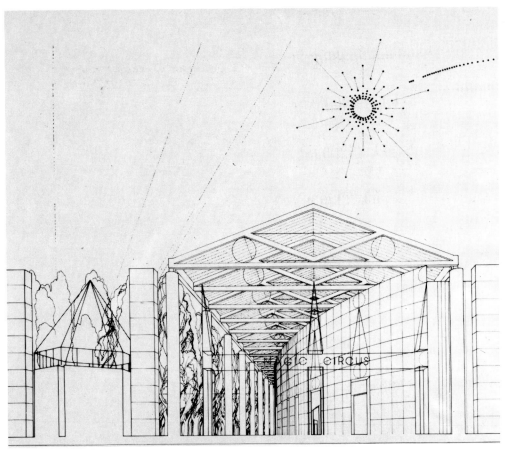

Francesco Cellini, competition for a theater, Forli, 1976.

Nicoletta Cosentino, project for the Agrarian Technical Institute, Maccarese, Rome, 1980.

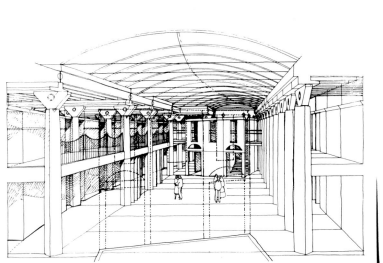

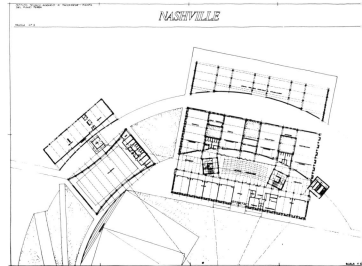

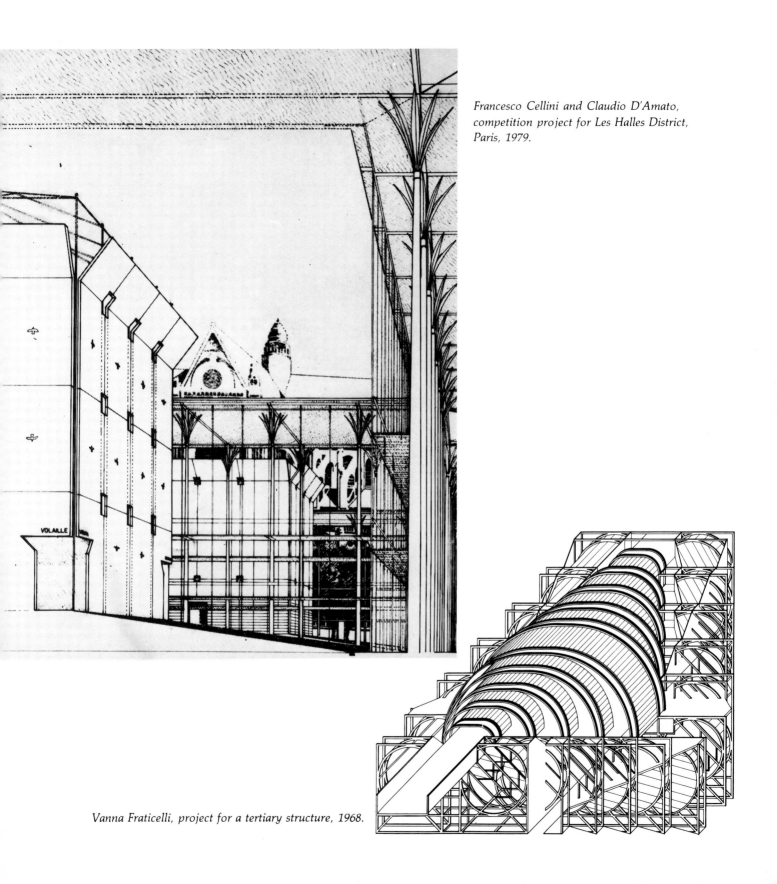

Francesco Cellini and Claudio D'Amato, competition project for Les Halles District, Paris, 1979.

Vanna Fraticelli, project for a tertiary structure, 1968.

Giampaolo Ercolani, project for university dining hall, Perugia, 1975.

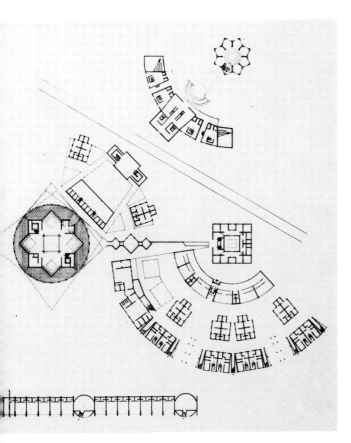

Claudio D'Amato, project for a middle school, Rome, 1967.

Stefano Caira and Vincenzo Sica, students of Claudio D'Amato, project for the layout of cultural activities, Latina, 1979.

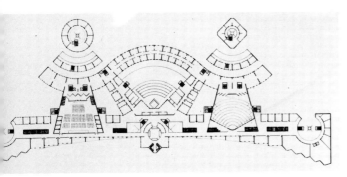

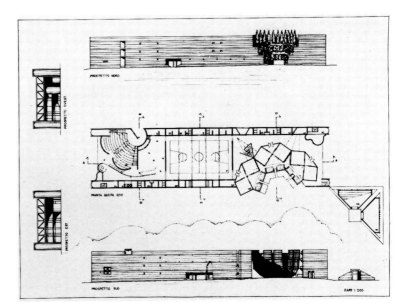

Mario Corsetti and Pasquale Mazzocchi, students of Claudio D'Amato, project for offices and commercial layout, Latina, 1979.

Luigi Caruso, project for the Agrarian Technical Institute, Maccarese, Rome, 1980.

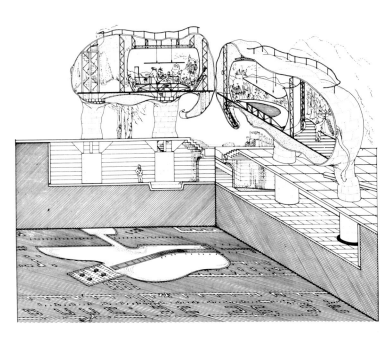

Pierluigi Nicolin and Italo Rota, project for Piazza Stamira, Ancona, 1978.

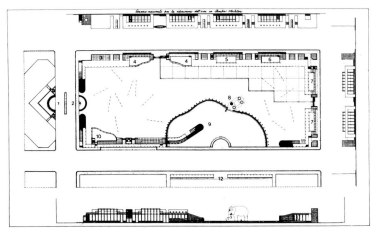

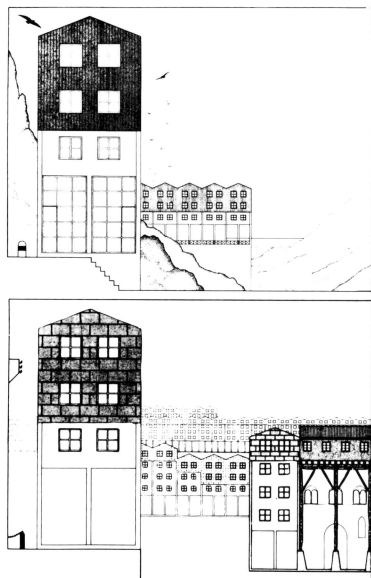

Claudio Baldisseri, Giuseppe Grossi, Bruno Minardi, competition project for housing, Foggia, 1976.

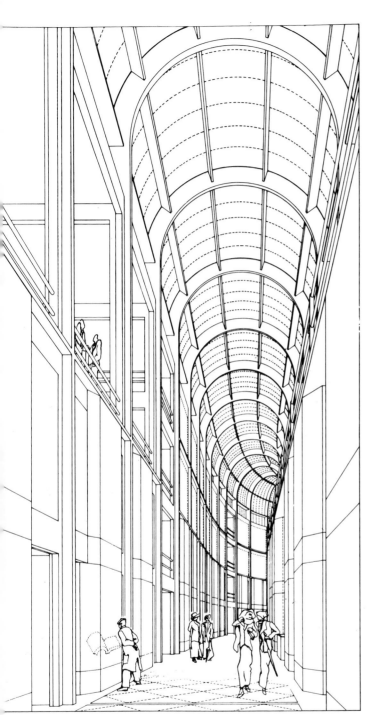

LEFT AND BELOW:
James Stirling, Civic Center, Derby, 1970.

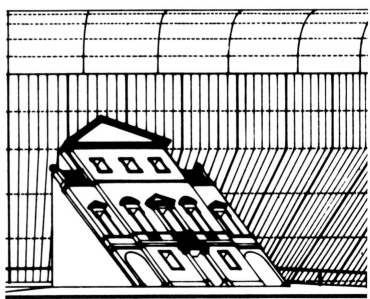

Francesco Cellini, Aleph House, Bracciano, Rome, 1972–77.

Francesco Cellini, Aleph House, Bracciano, Rome, 1972–77.

Francesco Cellini, Aleph House, Bracciano, Rome, 1972–77.

Francesco Cellini, Aleph House, Bracciano, Rome, 1972–77.

Jeremy and Fenella Dixon, project for apartment houses.

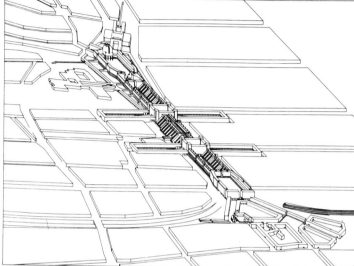

Léon Krier, project for new European Common Market District, Luxembourg, 1978.

Léon Krier, project for the new European Common Market District, Luxembourg, 1978.

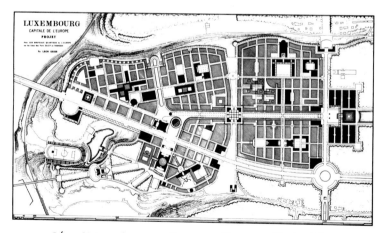

Léon Krier, plan, new European Common Market District, Luxembourg, 1978.

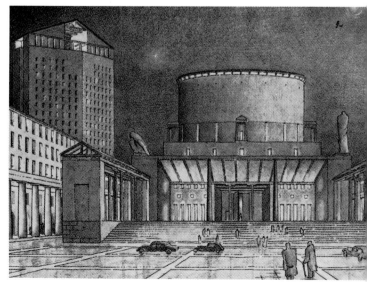

LEFT:

*Rob Krier, drawing for a square,
Leinfelden City Center,
near Stuttgart, 1971.*

*Rob Krier, perspective view
of Leinfelden City Center,
near Stuttgart, 1971.*

*Léon Krier, project for the
restoration of the inner city,
Echternach, 1970.*

S. Birkiye and G. Busieau, project for the reconstruction of Crossroads of Europe, Brussels, 1978.

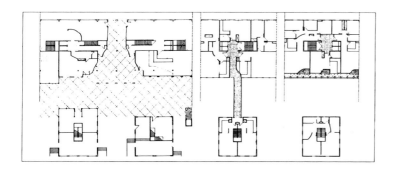

S. Birkiye, G. Busieau, P. Neirinck, project for a neighborhood restoration, Brussels, 1978.

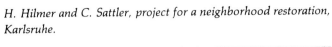

H. Hilmer and C. Sattler, project for a neighborhood restoration, Karlsruhe.

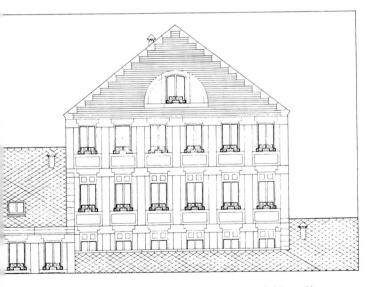

D. Ange, R. de Gernier, A. Lambrichs, project for restoration of a working class neighborhood, Brussels, 1978.

Charles Vandenhove, project for restoration of Hors-Chateau District, Liege, 1979.

H. Hilmer and C. Sattler, project for a neighborhood restoration, Karlsruhe.

ABOVE, BELOW AND BELOW RIGHT:
J.P. Kleihues with R. Hauser, project for museum, Blankenheim, 1976.

J.P. Kleihues, project for a pavilion at "Documenta 77," Kassel, 1976.

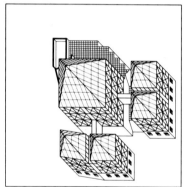

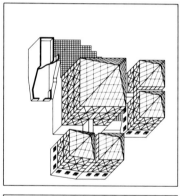

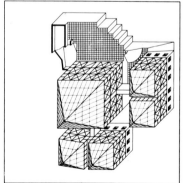

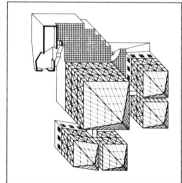

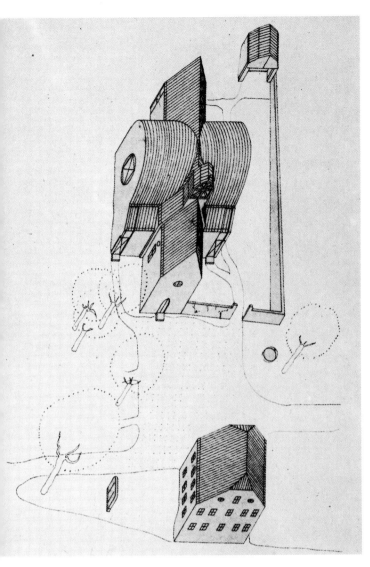

Heinz Tesar, project for a church, 1977.

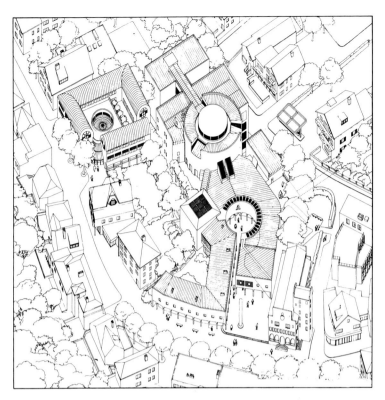

Gustav Peichl, axonometric view, project for museum, Vaduz, Leichtenstein.

Jean-Francois Laurent, competition project for a housing block, New Town of Cergy-Pontoise.

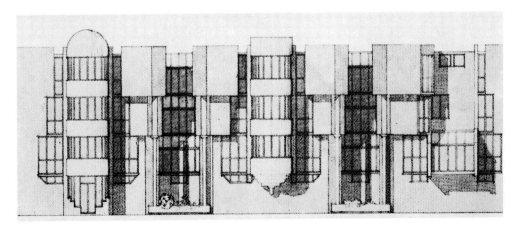

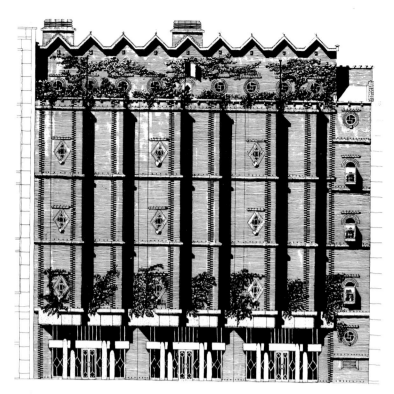

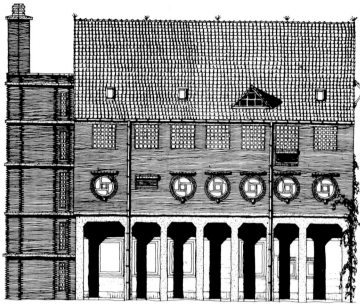

Rudiger Vael, project for an addition to telephone company headquarters, Grobbendonk.

Rudiger Vael, project for the central headquarters, telephone company, Anversa, 1977.

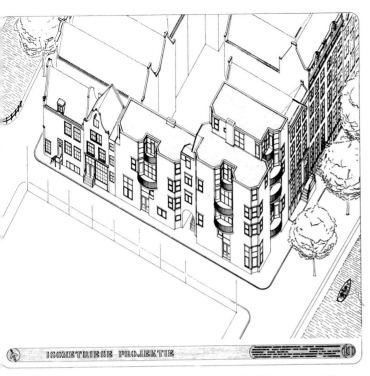

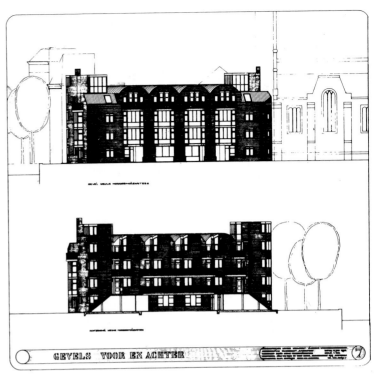

Aldo van Eyck and Theo Bosch, project for the Nieuwmarkt District, Amsterdam, 1975.

Aldo van Eyck and Theo Bosch, project for the Nieuwmarkt District, Amsterdam, 1975.

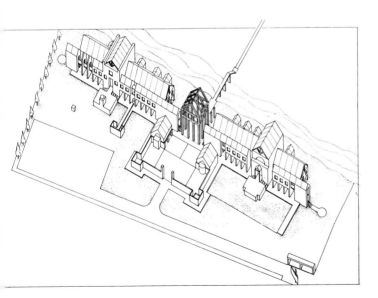

Fernando Montes, project for twin houses, Saint-Louis, Alto Reno, 1979.

Pancho Ayguavives, project for two houses on the coast of Normandy.

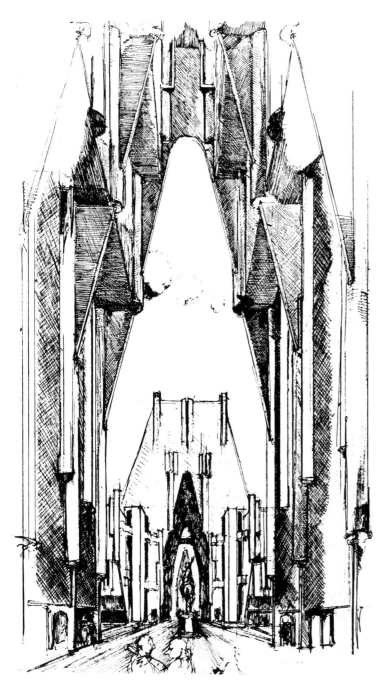

*Taller de Arquitectura, project for a residential complex,
"La petite Cathédrale," New Town of Cergy-Pontoise,
1971.*

*Taller de Arquitectura, project for the Meritxel Bridge,
Andorra, 1974.*

Taller de Arquitectura, "Marca Hispanica" Park, Le Perthus, 1975–78.

Lluis Clotet and Oscar Tusquets, Vittoria House, Pantelleria, 1973–75.

Lluis Clotet and Oscar Tusquets, detail, Belvedere Georgina, Llorfiu, Gerona, 1972.

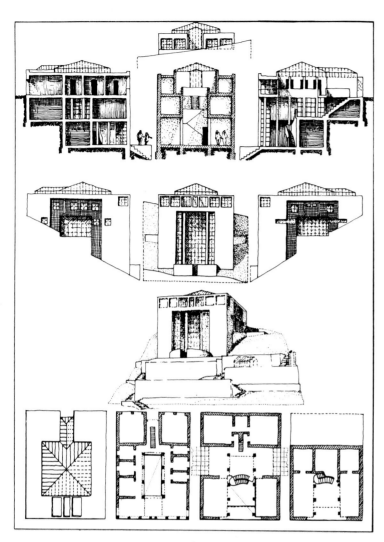

Rob Krier, project for Weidemann House, Stuttgart, 1975.

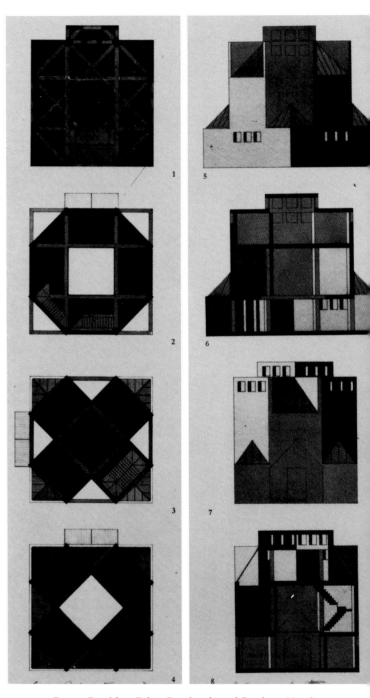

Bruno Reichlin, Fabio Reinhardt and Pierluigi Nicolin, project for Rivola House, Rivera, Ticino Canton.

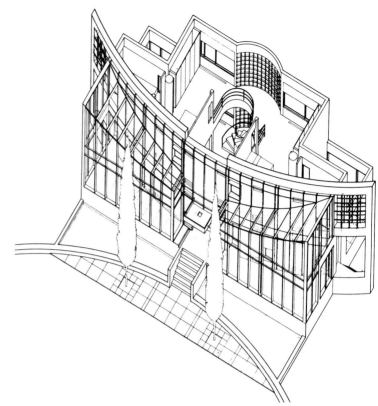

Diana Agrest and Mario Gandelsonas, project for a vacation house, Punta del Este, Uruguay, 1977.

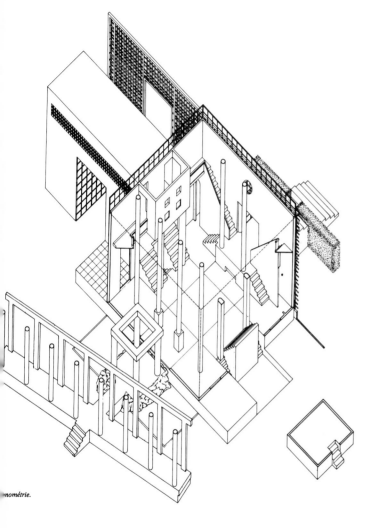

nométrie.

Warren Schwartz and Robert Silver, project for a small villa.

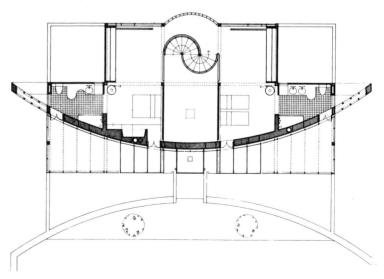

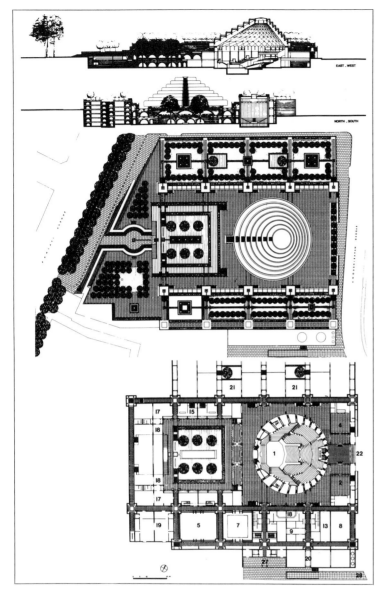

The Mandala Collaborative, detail, model, National Music Center, Teheran.

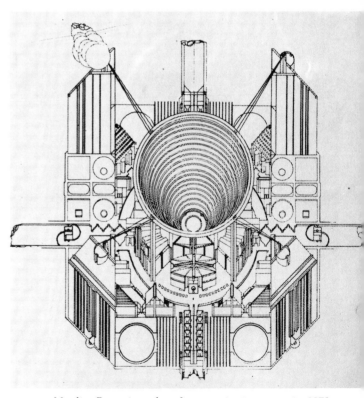

The Mandala Collaborative, project for National Music Center, Teheran.

Manlio Brusatin, plan for a suburban temple, 1970.

Yasufumi Kijima, pavilion, Kumamoto City, 1975.

ABOVE AND BELOW:
Yasufumi Kijima, interior of Zen Temple.

Yasufumi Kijima, layout of park, Shirakawa.

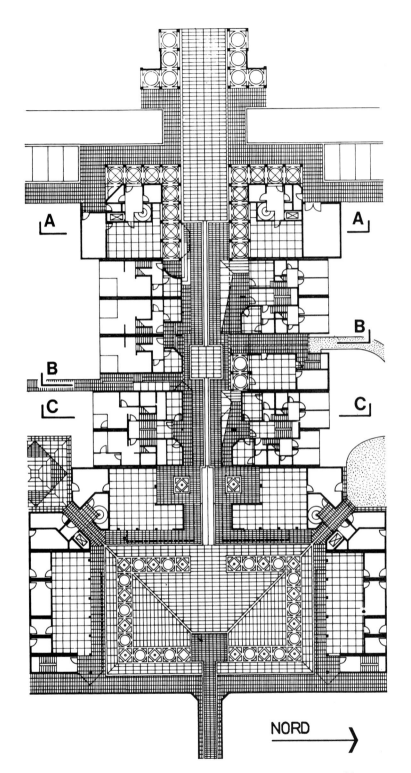

NORD ⟶

Ngyen-Huu, Zbduniewer, plan for competition project, New Town of Cergy-Pontoise.

B. Huet, D. Bigelman and S. Santelli, competition project for La Villette, Paris, 1975.

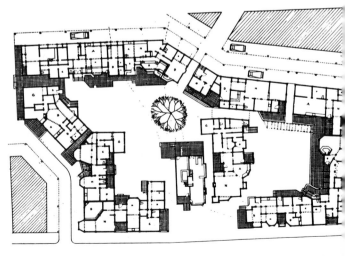

Christopher Alexander, plan for an apartment complex.

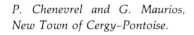
*Ngyen-Huu, Zbudniewer, three
perspective views of New Town of
Cergy-Pontoise.*

*P. Chenevrel and G. Maurios,
New Town of Cergy-Pontoise.*

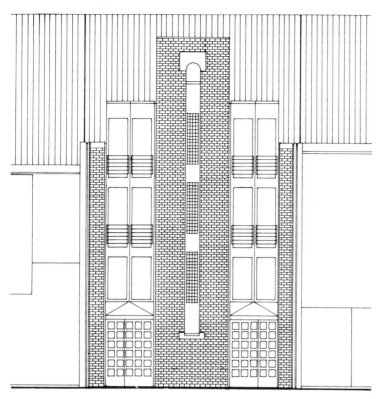

Wolfgang Doring, house, Kennedy Damm, Dusseldorf.

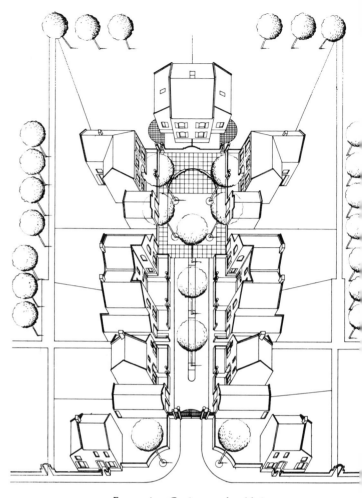

Francois Ceria and Alain Coupel, axonometric plan, Plan de L'Eglise, New Town of St-Quentin-en-Yvelines.

Barton Myers and Associates, project for Ghent Plaza, Norfolk, Virginia.

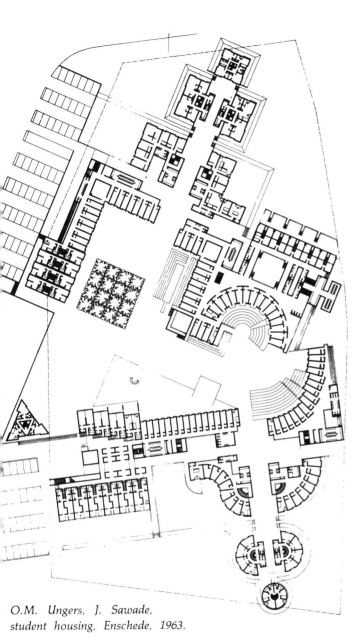

O.M. Ungers, J. Sawade,
student housing, Enschede, 1963.

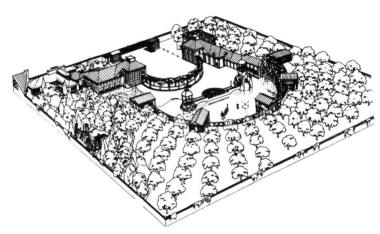

Christopher Luchsinger, competition project, Karl–Friedrich
Schinkel House, 1979.

Charles Moore, FAIA, William Hersy, John Kyrk, perspective and elevation, competition project, Karl–Friedrich
Schinkel House, 1979.

BIBLIOGRAPHY

AA.VV., *Architettura razionale*, Milan (no date).

A. Anselmi, *Occasioni d'architettura*, Rome 1980.

G. C. Argan, *Ignazio Gardella*, Milan 1959.

C. Aymonino, *Il significato delle città*, Rome-Bari 1975.

A. Barey, *Déclaration de Bruxelles*, Brussels 1978.

D. Bell, *The Coming of Post-Industrial Society: A Venture in Social Forecasting*, New York 1973.

A. Belluzzi, *La « ripetizione differente » nell'architettura di Robert Venturi*, Bologna (no date).

G. Benamo, *Rue des Hautes-Formes*, in « L'architecture d'aujourd'hui », n. 202, Paris 1979.

M. Benamou & Ch. Caramello, *Performance in Postmodern Culture*, Wisconsin 1977.

P. Blake, *Form Follows Fiasco*, Boston-Toronto 1974.

K. C. Bloomer & C. W. Moore, *Body, Memory and Architecture*, New Haven and London 1977.

R. Boyd, *Orientamenti nuovi nell'architettura giapponese*, New York and Milan 1969.

B. C. Brolin, *The Failure of Modern Architecture*, London 1976.

D. Canter, *The Psychology of Place*, London 1977.

A. Cappabianca, *Distruggere l'architettura*, Rome 1978.

C. Conforto, G. de Giorgi, A. Muntoni, M. Pazzaglini, *Il dibattito architettonico in Italia 1945-1975*, Rome 1977.

C. Dardi, *Semplice lineare complesso*, Rome 1976.

G. De Carlo, *Corpo, memoria e fiasco*, in « Spazio e società », n. 4, Milan 1978.

V. De Feo, *Il piacere dell'architettura*, Rome 1976.

R. De Fusco, *Storia dell'architettura contemporanea*, voll. I e II, Rome-Bari 1974.

C. De Seta, *Origini ed eclisse del movimento moderno*, Rome-Bari 1980.

D. Dunster, *Venturi and Rauch*, London 1978.

P. Eisenman, M. Graves, C. Gwathmey, J. Hejduk & R. Meier, *Five Architects*, New York 1972.

R. Filson, *La fuente magica de la Piazza d'Italia*, in « Arquitectura », n. 215, Madrid 1978.

I. Hassan, *The Dismemberment of Orpheus: Toward a Post-Modern Literature*, New York 1971.

R. Hughes, *U. S. Architects, Doing Their Own Thing*, in « Time », New York, January 1979.

A. Izzo & C. Gubitosi, *James Stirling*, Rome 1976.

C. Jencks & G. Baird, *Il significato in architettura*, London 1969, Bari 1974.

C. Jencks, *The Language of Post-modern Architecture*, London 1977.

C. Jencks, *Bizarre Architecture*, London 1979.

P. Johnson, *Writings*, New York 1979.

J. P. Kleihues, *En la encrucjada de la arquitectura alemana*, in « Construccion de la ciudad », n. 9, Barcelona 1977.

M. Kohler, *Postmodernismus: ein begriffgeschichtlicher Ueberblick*, 1977.

K. Kraus, *Detti e contraddetti*, Munich 1955, and Milan 1972.

R. Krier, *Stuttgart*, Stuttgart 1975.

J. F. Lyotard, *La condition postmoderne*, Paris 1979.

M. McLuhan, *The Mechanical Bride: Folklore of Industrial Man*, New York 1951.

C. Moore & G. Allen, *Dimensions*, New York 1976.

C. Moore, G. Allen, D. Lyndon, *The Place of Houses*, New York-Chicago-San Francisco 1974.

S. Muratori, *Architettura e civiltà in crisi*, Rome 1963.

P. Navone, B. Orlandoni, *Architettura « radicale »*, Segrate 1974.

C. Norberg Schulz, *Existence, Space and Architecture*, London 1971, Rome 1975.

C. Norberg Schulz, *Alla ricerca dell'architettura perduta*, Rome 1975.

C. Norberg Schulz, *Genius Loci. Paesaggio ambiente architettura*, Milan 1979.

W. Pehnt, *Neue deutsche Architektur 3*, Stuttgart 1970.

P. Portoghesi, *Le inibizioni dell'architettura moderna*, Rome-Bari 1974.

P. Portoghesi, *Il sistema industriale deve fare i conti con la natura*, in « L'Avanti », 18-11-1978.

P. Portoghesi, *L'architettura del futuro? È già nata alcuni secoli fa*, in « Euro », n. 2, Rome 1978.

P. Portoghesi, *La città alienata*, in « Almanacco socialista '79 ».

P. Portoghesi, *Tante case astratte per un uomo senza dimensioni*, in « La Repubblica », April 19, 1979.

P. Portoghesi, *Per una riprogettazione delle citta esistenti*, in « Mondoperaio », n. 6, Rome 1979.

P. Portoghesi, *Architettura del GRAU*, in « Controspazio », n. 1-2, Bari 1979.

F. Purini, *Luogo e progetto*, Rome 1976.

F. Purini, *Alcune forme della casa*, Rome 1979.

C. Ray Smith, *Supermannerism*, New York 1977.

C. Rowe, *Mannerism and Modern Architecture*, in « Architectural Review », May 1950.

V. Savi, *L'architettura di Aldo Rossi*, Milan 1976.

V. Scully, *The Shingle Style Today*, New York 1974.

V. Scully, *Louis I. Kahn*, New York 1962.

P. F. Smith, *Architecture and the Human Dimension*, London 1979.

R. Stern, *Orientamenti nuovi nell'architettura americana*, New York and Milan 1970.

M. Tafuri, F. Dal Co, *Architettura contemporanea*, Milan 1976.

M. Tafuri, *La sfera e il labirinto. Avanguardie e architettura da Piranesi agli anni '70*, Turin 1980.

M. Tafuri, *L'éphémère est eternel. Aldo Rossi a Venezia*, in « Domus », n. 602, Milan 1980.

H. Tesar, *Vorformen, Entwürfe, Verwirklichungen*, Vienna 1978.

A. Touraine, *La société Postindustrielle*, Denoel 1969. « Traverses », n. 4, Paris 1976. Numero monografico, *Functionalismes en dérive*.

R. Venturi, *Complexity and Contradiction in Architecture*, New York 1966.

R. Venturi, D. Scott Brown, S. Izenour, *Learning from Las Vegas*, Cambridge, Massachussets, 1972, London 1977.

B. Zevi, *Il linguaggio moderno dell'architettura*, Turin 1973.

Exhibition Catalogues

Aldo Rossi. Progetti e disegni 1962-1979, exhibition at Pan Gallery, Roma Aprile 1979. Directed by F. Moschini.

Aspetti dell'arte contemporanea, exhibition at Castello Cinquecentesco, L'Aquila 1963.

Assenza/presenza: un'ipotesi per l'architettura, exhibition at Galleria comunale d'arte moderna, Bologna 1977.

10 Immagini per Venezia, exhibition of projects for Cannareggio Ovest, Ala Napoleonica, Venice, April 1980, Directed by F. Dal Co.

Europa / America / Architetture urbane alternative suburbane, Biennial, Venice 1978. Directed by F. Raggi.

Nuovi disegni per il mobile italiano, Milan 1960.

Paolo Portoghesi. Progetti e disegni 1949-1979, Florence 1979. Directed by F. Moschini.

Per una simbolica dell'ambiente, Venice 1978.

Roma interrotta, exhibition at Mercati Traianei, Rome 1978.

Topologia e morfogenesi, Biennial, Venice 1978. Directed by L. V. Masini.

Transformations in Modern Architecture, New York 1979. Directed by A. Drexler.

Magazines

Too much space would be required to enumerate all the contributions to the debate on post-modern architecture. We will limit ourselves, therefore, to suggesting that our readers consult the magazines which have published the most significant critical contributions to the discussion of resolutions to the crisis of the modern movement:

A + U , Tokyo.

A M C , Paris.

Architectural Design , London.

Archives d'architecture moderne , Brussels.

Arquitectura , Madrid.

Controspazio , Rome.

Construccion de la ciudad , Barcelona.

L'architecture d'aujourd'hui , Paris.

Lotus , Milan.

Opposition , New York.

Process , Tokyo.

Werk-Archithese , Zurich.